MIMESIS
INTERNATIONAL

PHILOSOPHY

n. 66

Roberto Pujia

BERTRAND RUSSELL'S IDEALIST HERITAGE

A Neglected Legacy

© 2024—Mimesis International
www.mimesisinternational.com
e-mail: info@mimesisinternational.com

Isbn: 9788869774744
Book series: *Philosophy*, n. 66

© MIM Edizioni Srl
P.I. C.F. 02419370305

CONTENTS

To Angelica and Margherita
two 'things of beauty' and 'joys forever'

FOREWORD

This enquiry here republished in a new revised edition is not meant to be a survey of Russell's philosophical thought, or an attempt at a systematic overview of his philosophy, it aims, only, to contribute to a more balanced interpretation of some focal topics of his research on theory of knowledge and the relationship between language and experience.

Although contemporary thought and in particular those philosophers who, in various ways, fall within the so-called linguistic turn have in Russell one of the most significant and fruitful inspirers and interpreters, his overall conception of the ends and methods of philosophy falls, rather, within the classical tradition of western thought; that one according to which formal deduction is or mirrors actual deduction and sees philosophy as the search for truth.

The furrow that separates Russell from the so called 'second' Wittgenstein and, above all, his followers is not so much to be found in the different techniques of language analysis as in their theoretical foundation. Whereas for Wittgenstein's followers and successors the analysis of symbolism, once lost the cognitive value of philosophy, is self-validating, it is, conversely, for Russell, only a tool for representing and grasping non-linguistic reality. The Russellian claim is the same of Plato and Aristotle. On these ontological assumptions rest, as we shall see, his theory of meaning and his logic in general.

A proper interpretation of Russell's philosophy cannot, consequently, disregard or underestimate an exposition of its links with the earlier tradition that also reveals its original contribution, but this claim would represent only a flat platitude if Russell's relations with the classical tradition had not been, as we shall see, neglected if not obscured in various ways.

I tried, thus, to highlight not only the complex web of relations that binds Russell's thought to the empiricist tradition but also the more neglected ones that link it directly or otherwise to other streams of thought such as idealism (at least in the original version it took on in England especially through the work by F. H. Bradley).

While, in fact, Russell's debt to empiricism has been extensively investigated, a somehow hasty assumption of idealist thought as a mere polemical target of its realist pluralism has seriously harmed a comprehensive assessment of Russell's connections and influences. Thus a source of his logic and theory of knowledge has been obscured, to illustrate which, layers of prejudice should now be overcome.

I tried to show that it is possible to document a direct incidence of idealist thought on Russell's philosophy, attempting to subtract it from a reading of it as something, rising in a sort of vacuum.

The variety and complexity of Russell's work is so overwhelming, not to be easily mastered other than within a strict thematic perimeter and circumscription and the adoption of strict interpretive criteria. In this essay, therefore, only a period running from the beginnings to 1918 is examined, with some detail. As for interpretive criteria there I see two basic points of reference in the study of Russellian philosophy: the first is the complex issue, already mentioned, of relations within the English empiricist and non-empiricist tradition. The effort to place the English philosopher in a proper historical perspective, in balance between the empiricist tradition and the renewal of this tradition, the recovery and reconstruction of thematic and methodological links that appear at first sight quite improbable allow, in many cases, a better assessment of the theoretical coherence of some of his contributions.

As for the second criterion, I think that it is represented by the need to keep constantly in mind, as a focus, an element intrinsic to his philosophy whose centrality, represents a kind of ground zero that reflects all peripheral changes. It is the theory of meaning. The continuous, successive changes in his thought are always. or almost always, consequences or causes of the change in his theory of meaning which I think underlies, all his ontology and theory of knowledge and for which it acts as a kind of "ghost in the machine."

R.P.
Rome
February 2024

ACKNOWLEDGMENTS

Far too many are the people to whom I am in various ways intellectually and personally indebted to be able to acknowledge them all here. I'll therefore shrink to three of them who in a kind of roadmap shaped my scholar life. I feel, first and foremost an enormous gratitude for Gabriele Baldini, a true master whose unparalleled passionate scholarship combined with to a truly rare elegance of writing and mesmerizing teaching skills displayed to me the beauty and richness of English literature, art and culture at large. A bit later as a young philosophy graduate student I had the unvaluable chance to meet at Queen's in Oxford Brian McGuinness, whose immense knowledge guided me since then – with his peculiar formal elegant trait – on my journey through the winding paths of English analytic philosophy, especially through Moore's, Russell's and Wittgenstein's thought and accompanied my research for many, many years. Finally, I have to remember someone to whom I feel particularly grateful in a unique way: Rosaria Egidi, first my teacher and then my colleague, who for almost my whole life has continued to honour me with her friendship and continues even today to be an example of doctrine and unfailing rigour in research. Finally I would like to express my warmest thanks to Linda Valle for the acribic help in the editing of this work.

CHAPTER ONE
IDEALISM IN NINETEENTH CENTURY
BRITISH CULTURE

Entry and assimilation of idealism

Bertrand Russell has been a great innovator; with Gottlob Frege and George Moore, he shares the paternity of a turning point that imprinted contemporary thought with a radical, paradigmatic change; a turning point that involved both the object and the method of philosophical research, at least in English-speaking countries, and made analysis of language the core of research.

The strong anti-speculative character of late mid two thousand century, Anglo-Saxon philosophy and the focusing of philosophical enquiry to an eminently analytical "practice" owe much to his contribution as a matrix that is, at the same time, indubitable and ambiguous. The ambiguity lies in the fact that while Russell provided contemporary thought with a technical (i.e. logical) toolkit for analysing language, which thereupon became the heritage of so-called *analytic philosophy*, and indeed became a philosophy itself, nonetheless he himself never considered philosophy as a mere analysis of language, independent or apparently independent of an underlying ontology. Quite the contrary; in fact, he shares all the limitations and ambiguities arising from the uncomfortable position between two ways of thinking, two very different and, very often, mutually incongruent sensibilities, which rather than facing each other, cannot actually interact due to the absence of a common ground; due, in turn, to a sort of thematic and methodological asymmetry. Russell swings between a conception of philosophy as an ontology and on another side to its reduction to a methodology, a practice; between the classical aspiration for knowledge of the ultimate reality of things and the more modest intention to amend language from misleading expressions; participating in both tendencies. So that any attempt to explain his personality and work by reducing it to, or even only exalting its methodological and logical component, i.e. by attempting an assimilation to the new philosophy that he certainly contributed to arouse, returns an inadequate image of the development of his thought. A thought that may appear unintelligible if deprived of its traditional and classical component. Just as an adequate understanding of, say, Galilei's work requires to focus its neo-Platonic components on a *par with* the innovative specificities of his method, one would not understand and explain the sort of 'revolt against the father' that subsequent philosophical analysts, especially the Oxonians, have waged against Russell[1] if we shed some light only over the innovative aspects, neglecting or even underestimating either his ties with the classical tradition of empiricism, (of which he is, in some way, the extreme expression), or the weight – much more relevant than commonly believed – exerted, in the economy of his thought, by its idealist novitiate and, above all, by Bradley's lesson. Thus, while his thinking is at the origin of the subsequent philosophy of language with the centrality of language in philosophical research, he cannot, strictly speaking, be considered a philosopher of language, unless we give this expression a broader meaning that very few philosophers of language would be willing to subscribe to today.

In addition to its reductive character no longer accepted, linguistic analysis does not, in Russell's philosophy, exhaust the entire methodological and thematic horizon of research', nor does it constitute an autonomous and independent province, but rather a method that, being rooted on a ground of metaphysical presuppositions, represents a tool to be used in the broader enterprise of understanding reality. And this approach makes him

---

1   I refer to the rejection of the so-called reductive analysis of language and the application of a descriptive or therapeutic analysis, inspired above all by the work of what once was referred to as the "second" Wittgenstein as practised by the philosophers of the Oxford school. On the transition from one analytical perspective to the other see the illuminating essay by James O.Urmson, *Philosophical Analysis*

a metaphysician, related, as has often been said, more to Locke and Hume than to Wittgenstein's followers.[2]

This peculiar position also accounts for both the intertwisted tangle of logical and metaphysical analysis and the presence in his thought of fundamental assumptions that, though not always made explicit, constantly exert their influence.

The philosophical relevance of linguistic analysis – conceived as an investigation into the logical structure of utterances – is rooted in the metaphysical assumption that the structure of reality is somehow mirrored in the structure of language, so that the explication of the structure of language is the means to tap into the true nature of extralinguistic reality. The development of an analytical methodological perspective is thus historically part of the attempt to renew the pluralist realism of Locke, Hume, Stuart Mill, overcoming, however, the limitations that the neo-idealist critique had highlighted and which, as we shall see, Russell treasured. He too, moreover, embraced. albeit briefly, Bradley's anti-empiricist neo-Hegelianism, later distancing himself from it because of its alleged inability to agree with common sense and science. The application of logical analysis thus matured on the ground of the refutation of the ontological monism inherent in English idealism. A refutation that, as I shall try to show, did not prevent Russell from appropriating and bending the lesson received to his original position.

When in October 1890 Russell entered Cambridge, at the age of eighteen, he had no specific philosophical training behind him, although he had already begun a few years earlier solitary reflections originated from the need for an objective verification of religious beliefs and the foundations of mathematics. Mathematics at this time was for him a complex interest in which motives of a different order converged. While on the one hand it satisfied the intellect with the pure exercise of deductive rigour, and with the satisfaction coming from the certainty of its judgements, it also provided him with a capital methodological interest stemming from the youthful belief that nature operates according to strict laws. Nor did he

---

2   On Russell's general conception of the ends of philosophical research see Alfred Julius Ayer, *Russell and Moore,* p.10.

find the empiricist interpretation of mathematical propositions as empirical generalisations totally satisfactory if, as he recalls, he finally overcame his disappointment for the fact that one had to start its study with the acceptance of indemonstrable postulates.[3] Nor more satisfying appeared to him the empiricist interpretation of mathematical propositions as empirical generalizations, although Stuart Mill, whose works he read before entering university, was the thinker he felt most congenial to him. The propensity for empiricism was, however, to be temporarily tarnished by subsequent influences. Russell dedicated the first three Cambridge years to the study of mathematics and it was his interest in the problems relating to its foundation, as well as the decisive influence of Moore, that would definitively launch him into philosophical reflection, at the same time distancing him from the idealism that triumphed at Oxford in those years and that his work would contribute decisively to supplanting. His idealist interlude spans four years between 1894 and 1898. During this period all the influences he was undergoing moved in the direction of German idealism, or rather, of that particular form of idealism that developed in England between the middle of the 19th century and the first twenty years of the current one and that reached full theoretical maturity with the works of McTaggart, Bosanquet and, above all, Bradley with whom, as we shall see, Russell entertained a long and interesting debate. Initial vehicles of these influences were James Ward and especially McTaggart, who were not long in overcoming the 'rather coarse' empiricism that had until then satisfied him. After the first three years of mathematical studies Russell devoted the fourth year to philosophy and in 1894 considered himself "Hegelian to the marrow". A Kant-inspired essay on the foundations of geometry[4] and another on the relations between number and quantity belong to this phase.[5] The one and the other were to be part of a broader plan

---

3   B. Russell, 'My Mental Development' p. 7.
4   Russell, B. *An Essay on the Foundations of Geometry* (Cambridge: Cambridge University Press, 1897)
5   Russell, B. 'On the Relations of Number and Quantity', *Mind,* v. 6, (1896), 326-341

including, on the one hand, writings on the philosophy of science, in order to increase concreteness, from mathematics to biology, *and.* on the other, works on political and social subjects in order to increase abstractness. The whole was then to converge in a Hegelian synthesis that would "combine theory and praxis together" This project, as subsequent developments testify, was to be abandoned shortly afterwards. In 1898, some essays by Moore opened a breach in his idealist thought and Russell would follow the path that would soon lead him to his own autonomous philosophical position, the first emergence of which might be seen in a controversy with Bradley that was to continue for many years and was consummated, rather than resolved, only with the latter's death.[6]

The controversy that has long pitted Russell against Bradley presents at least two major reasons for interest. While from the point of view of the former's personal philosophical vicissitude it constitutes the ground on which his intellectual autonomy matured and is therefore to be seen as a necessary moment for understanding the subsequent developments of his thought, on a historical level, it fits into the broader framework of the penetration, flowering and subsequent decline in English culture of idealist thought inspired by Kantian and Hegelian German philosophy.

This British philosophy season, spanning between the work of Coleridge and that of Bradley, is a fascinating field of research and study, especially because of the influence it exerted on pluralist thinkers and, in general, albeit indirectly, on philosophies inspired by the analysis of language. It seems that its effects have been and still appear to be a bit neglected. Many questions remain still unanswered and many problems unsolved, such as the relationship between native and imported components of English idealism. Thus, although the analysis of this chapter of the history of thought is not really among the direct and immediate aims of this essay, an examination of some of its salient features and main lines of development is remarkably rewarding and in some cases even necessary to fully understand the

---

6   A controversy that recalls the famous Joseph Conrad's short novel *The Duel*. A story of a lifelong fight! Cf. Joseph Conrad, *The Duel*. Russell and Conrad were close friends.

links of some significant components of early Russell's philosophy with a tradition usually underestimated.

So well-established by now is the belief (but perhaps it would be more accurate to speak of prejudice) that identifies 'English philosophy' with the empiricist thought that runs from Bacon to Hume, that the albeit significant works of individual thinkers or even of "schools" not referable to this tradition in various ways are mostly considered exceptions that confirm the fundamental empiricist 'natural bias' a kind of national genius. Certainly, at first sight, it cannot but be astonishing that the idealist metaphysics and gnoseology, so peculiar in method and content, of the German tradition and culture have not only crossed the English Channel, but penetrated and rooted in Anglo-Saxon thought so tenaciously as to express themselves not only in more or less isolated epigones, but in a proper school that, after an initial phase of popularisation of Kant's Schelling's and Hegel's work, developed soon after a largely original and autonomous thought that, rapidly conquered academic circles, and was to exert a profound influence not only on culture but on the customs and on the political and social life of the entire country; and this thanks to the function as a forge for the education of the ruling class exercised by the two universities of Cambridge and Oxford; and then, on a more general level, because of the close link that has always existed in England between philosophical research, cultural debate on the one hand and social and political debate on the other.

A slightly closer examination reveals, nonetheless, that idealist thought is anything but foreign to English culture and traditions and that the English idealist renaissance of the 19th century cannot be entirely resolved or explained by the *tout court* penetration of German speculation, even if this is its priority component.[7] Two distinct elements converge in English idealism, without always succeeding in composing themselves in a unitary synthesis: on the one hand, the Platonic tradition that goes back to John Scotus Eriugena and that draws its maximum speculative vigour in the 17th century with the Cambridge Neo-Platonists, continuing afterwards with Berkeley, J.

---

7   A general view on the development of British idealism can be found in
     Jean -Paul Rosaye, *F.H. Bradley et l'idealisme britannique* 2020)

Norris and Collier and, on the other hand, the German Kantian and post-Kantian idealism introduced into England at the beginning of the 19th century. German thought, in short, did not invade and disrupt the British tradition but rather grafted itself onto its secondary trunk which, although overwhelmed by the greater vitality of empiricism, had never ceased to be present in English culture.

The presence of those two factors explains the specific character of British neo-idealism and the consideration of the alternating prevalence of one and the other is perhaps a key to its interpretation. This explains, also, the peculiar interest of the British idealists for ethical and religious problems, although the logical component is far from being absent and, for the purposes of our enquiry, seems to be the most important one, and shows certain fundamental divergences from Hegelian thought present even in the most Hegelian of its exponents: Bradley and McTaggart. Among the most significant divergences, it is worth mentioning some extremely peculiar ones that characterise the British idealists. Firstly, they all rejected *contradiction* as the driving element of the dialectic. Although with different emphasis, *contradiction* was seen by McTaggart and later by Bradley not as a dynamic principle but as a sign of imperfection, revealed in the apparent multiplicity of reality. On this basis, the cognitive inability of the abstract intellect is consequently reaffirmed, arriving at a virtual statement of the incommensurability of thought and being: the former characterised by proceeding from term to term and the latter, the Absolute, unattainable by the former because it cannot be achieved as the final term of a relational chain, nor as the sum of parts.[8]

The most peculiar and specific trait, the one by which English idealism is distinguished and different from its German matrix and which betrays its Neo-Platonic origin, is its ideological and religious character. Benjamin Whichcote Provost of Cambridge's Kings College, Ralph Cudworth and the other Cambridge Neo-Platonists conceived philosophy as a rigorous and articulate expression of

---

8   On these issues see Harold. Joachim, *The Nature of Truth* (and John Passmore, *A Hundred Years of Philosophy* pp. 60 ff.; Richard Wollheim, *F. H. Bradley* pp. 90-91.

the ideas underlying religious experiences and intended to oppose the mechanistic conception of the world implicit in Cartesian philosophy[9]. Even in Berkeley's thought, after all, hovers the intention to lend a solid theoretical structure to the defences against the deism that underlay Newtonian physics and the very idealists, who were most inspired by German thought: those of the generation following Coleridge, as James Frederick Ferrier, James H. Stirling, Edward Caird and Th. H. Green who fought against the encroachment of materialism represented according to them by utilitarian ethics and Mill's philosophy. They provided, as James says, an almost metaphysical backbone to Puritan Christianity and social and economic liberalism.

It was not until the second half of the 19th century that began to develop in England a more systematic idealism in which certain methodological characteristics and criticisms of empiricist psychologism began to appear, and was not only to be preserved but was to constitute a very significant contribution to contemporary thought.

The subsequent realist and pluralist development of English thought, linked to the names of Russell, Moore and Wittgenstein, drawing on the great empiricist tradition, has perhaps buried, along with the condemnation of metaphysics, the memory of a methodological debt to idealism that deserves to be noted instead, and whose load will appear more clearly in the examination of certain methodological and doctrinal features of Russell's epistemology and logic.

To correct, therefore, the widespread belief according to which contemporary analytical currents and those focused on language analysis constitute flowers in the desert, it may help to identify whether certain their peculiar methodological and theoretical constants should not be traced, more than generally recognised as significant contributions from different schools and trends. It is on

---

9   At first they accepted and shared Descartes' thought, which they interpreted as a barrier against empiricist attitudes and a victory against scholasticism, and only later did they turn away from it fearing that the process inherent in his physiology threatened the spiritual interpretation of the universe they advocated.

the basis of such hypothesis that it will be rewarding to investigate, albeit briefly, the modalities of the birth and development of English idealist thought, identifying some of its components that seem to reappear variously camouflaged in analytic philosophy in general and in Russell's philosophy in particular.

In the first half of the 19th century, the English philosophical landscape was widely characterised by the influence of Kantian thought on the indigenous trunk of Neo-Platonism; but it was only after 1865[10] that this influence was to be superimposed on it, without ever cancelling the first one that of Hegel.

This cultural transplant was not, however, to take place in a univocal and linear manner as a *tout-court* acquisition of critical philosophy. The multiplicity and cultural diversity of the protagonists of this operation considerably complicates the picture that is, in fact, incredibly thick with interpretations, misrepresentations, developments. In other words, it would be neither correct nor adequate to speak univocally of *the* English reading of Kant since the many readings were influenced by the individual personalities, even if this multiplicity would later tend to be reduced to a few dominant attitudes in the progressive passage from an initial phase of assimilation and diffusion to a subsequent one of synthesis, preparatory to autonomous developments.

It is precisely in the peculiar interpretation that Kantian critical philosophy had in England, in its encounter with the Scottish school and the neo-Platonic tradition on the one hand and Hegelian thought on the other, that the foundations of that critique of classical

---

10   That year was published *The Secret of Hegel.* by James H. Stirling, a Scottish doctor who had abandoned his profession for philosophy. This work would have a profound influence and certainly marks a milestone in the penetration of Hegelism in England. Despite all its 'imitations', it constitutes the first attempt at assimilation and confrontation with idealist thought. It is in essence a long commentary on the deduction of categories. Hegel's well-kept secret, according to Stirling's detractors, would reside in the concept of the *concrete universal* that, according to the theologising interpretation of idealism, provides the means for the synthesis and reconciliation of reason and faith, of sensibility and rational knowledge and, therefore, for overcoming the opposition between religious aspirations and rational needs.

empiricism must be sought that will substantiate much of Bradley's thought and will transcend, if not in its specific contents, into certain fundamental trends of that revision of empiricism which animates Russell's thought.

Although Kant's thought and mainly his first *Critique* began to be introduced in England fairly early – the miscellaneous volume by the Irish physician J.A.O'Keeffe that refers to it, dates from 1795[11] – a direct and in-depth knowledge of Criticism did not come about until the middle of the following century with William Hamilton and Henry Longueville Mansel. This time span includes a plethora of introductions, translations, commentaries and lectures,[12] the value of which, with a few exceptions, is for the most part very low, also and above all due to the personality of their authors: generally enthusiastic admirers lacking a specific philosophical background and the necessary interpretative tools to train in the exegesis of a text so difficult to assimilate. Such works were, moreover, quickly forgotten if not ignored at all and in any case left no trace in English thought. It is also within this framework, albeit at a certainly more relevant level if only because of the wide influence it exerted on subsequent generations of scholars, that we find Coleridge's writings and the lectures mentioned earlier.

Poets, writers and philosophers

The suture between the English Neo-Platonic tradition and German thought, that is, the initial moment of the idealist renaissance of the 19th century, is, according to some historians, the work of Samuel Taylor Coleridge, a work that is still much debated and on which the critics are far from unanimous. The debate obviously does not refer to the contribution of the poet and critic for which he is numbered among the greats of English literature, but that of the philosopher. It is difficult, on the other hand, to underestimate the influence and

---

11   In the work, entitled *An Essay on the Progress of Understanding, he quotes* passages from the *Critique of Pure Reason.*
12   A rich and keen review and discussion on these works can be found in Jean Pucelle, *Idealism en Angleterre,*pp. **88-89**

extraordinary consequences that his writings and lectures have exerted in several ways on English culture. The historical role of Coleridge's work had, moreover, been widely perceived as early as 1840 by John Stuart Mill who, in an essay on the philosopher-poet, while distancing himself from the contents of his speculation, expressed a substantial tribute of esteem by comparing him, beyond the different conceptions, to Bentham for the fecundity of his ideas.[13] The critical problem raised by Coleridge's work concerns therefore only its theoretical value and originality. While some, with J.H. Muirhead, maintain that in his writings we find, albeit in methodological disorder and in the acknowledged lack of systematicity, the elements of a personal doctrine and philosophy, to which his direct disciples, such as Th.H.Green, will only give a more organic arrangement[14] others affirm with R. Wellek[15] that his merits do not go beyond those of a brilliant disseminator of the thought of others and that, although Coleridge did not lack speculative ability and vast culture, he was driven back by his own systematic lability into a philosophy of faith-reason dualism in which the latter had to be necessarily subordinate to the former, so that the fragmentary elements of his doctrine would all go back to the Greeks, to the Neo-Platonists of the Cambridge school and above all to Kant and Schelling.

Coleridge, who fed his philosophical writings with obscure metaphors and daring neologisms was, fully aware of its shortcomings and of the gap never bridged between ends and methods. He, has, however, the merit of having, if not introduced, certainly contributed decisively to the diffusion of Kantian thought in England and in a certain sense is at the origin of the idealist rebirth. He will find in the philosopher of Königsberg, of whom he will give a reading, to say the

---

13 John. Stuart Mill, 'Bentham' in *London and Westminster Review,* August 1838 and 'Coleridge' in the March 1840 issue of the same journal. The two essays were brought together in a small volume entitled *Mill on Bentham and Coleridge* (London: Chatto & Windus, 1967. See pp. 99 ff. of this edition.

14 See, John H. Muirhead, *The Platonic Tradition in Anglo-Saxon Philosophy,* p. 14; 'Past and Present in Contemporary Philosophy' p. 310; see also Claud Howard, *Coleridge's idealism,* 1924)

15 Cf. René.Wellek, *Immanuel Kant in England,* 1793-1838 p. 67 ff.

least, singular and limiting, the complete and systematic expression of his confused and unconnected intuitions. Coleridge's Kantian reading is totally focused on the distinction between *Vernunft* and *Verstand*.[16]This dichotomy, which is the foundation of other pairs of opposites, pervades and permeates his entire philosophy and is extraordinarily important because it is the core from which will develop, with a very different theoretical rigour in the other idealists, the fundamental issue of the opposition between relative and absolute, part and whole, *appearance* and *reality* on which the subsequent monism is grounded. Of the Kantian distinction, Coleridge grasps only the negative and limiting aspect. Above all, he emphasises the narrowness and passivity of the intellect, bound to the world of phenomena and the logic of concepts, circumscribed by a space-time horizon, which is contrasted by reason as the highest expression of human freedom, doomed to intuitively grasp the absolute. The philosopher-poet will interpret, in other words, the *noumenon* (and this will become a *topos* of early Romantic idealism), not as a logical limit of knowability, but as the object of reason's intuitive knowledge, as distinct from the knowledge of the data in the space-time horizon to which the intellect is bound. Moreover unlike Kant, Coleridge ascribed a constitutive and not a regulative function to ideas. thus finalising, as says C. Howard[17] the Kantian logic to a fundamentally Platonic idealism. He intended above all to oppose the philosophers of the intellect, the empiricists, to whom he reproached the reduction of the vital to the mechanical, which, in his view, nullified human faith and freedom. The pluralist and realist conception of a world

---

16 The *terminus a quo* of Coleridge's approach to the German philosophers is unknown. However, the end of 1796 – the period in which he refers to Kant as the 'incomprehensible Immanuel Kant' in a letter – is to be taken into account, cf. John H.Muirhead, *Coleridge as a Philosopher,* p. 50. A more systematic study of Kant's philosophy would not begin until after 1801. The distinction between theoretical and practical reason is raised by Coleridge in *Friend,* 1808, where he contrasts the organ of the supersensible, 'the mind's eye' with the 'vis rationalis'. Cf. *Complete Works* II, pp. 145-6. However, it reappears in both *Biographia Literaria* (1817) and *Aids to Reflection* (1824-25). See also *Notebooks,* 26 BM Add MSS p. 22-3.

17 In the aforementioned *Coleridge's Idealism*

made up of parts seemed completely inconceivable to him. The organic whole, the whole, could not be reduced to the distributive whole, the sum (all). Empirical knowledge was generally condemned and qualified as pure appearance, (reopening, with incalculable theoretical consequences, which precisely with Bradley would come to fruition), the ancient dichotomy of appearance and reality, or else it was considered *useful for the sake of the* purpose, but not *true*.

The object of true knowledge is, instead, the absolute that reason grasps in an unanalysable act of intuition. The content of this doctrine both for the unfamiliarity and aptitude of Coleridge and basically the whole of English culture for the modalities of the German idealist dialectic, as well as for the not very strong theoretical temperament of the philosopher-poet, were expressed in an essentially rhapsodic and literary style that fed, as we have said, more on obscure metaphors and philosophical euphuisms than on speculative rigour. Other Romantics, on the other hand. suspicious of the unmotivated anti-scientific rebelliousness and uncertain about the theoretical soundness of such formulations, not only did not adhere to them but also took the opportunity to polemise with them, ridiculing their supporters. This was the case with Thomas L. Peacock who, in his novel *Melincourt*, takes pleasure with a subtle and exquisite satirical vein in making Coleridge play the role of Moley Mystic Esquire, a visionary who lives in Cimmerian Lodge, a mansion situated on the *Island of Pure Intellect,* in the middle of a swamp called the *Ocean of Deceptive Form* and surrounded by the thickest fog, through which he guides visitors using a "synthetic torch" that, by means of the *rays of transcendental illumination* (Kantian metaphysics), emanates the *visible darkness* and leads them into the *luminous dark*[18]. Moley's Mystic Esquire naturally despised any form of

---

18 It is interesting to note, in this regard, the indirect outlook that this satire provides of Coleridge's authentic and peculiar lexicon. In one place in *Notebook* 26 he argues that reason is used in two senses; intellectual (or scientific) and practical. In the former it might more conveniently be called *light* of reason (italics mine) instead of *reason* alone.

analytical or empirical knowledge that could be communicated to others outside of intuition.[19]

This sketchy picture of the penetration of idealism in England would, however, be not so much exhaustive as partially adequate if a further, albeit indirect, component were not taken into account. An off-course entry representing a different viewpoint according to which the idealist currents were not in crisis at the turn of the century in England and that Bradley contribution has not been neglected nor did not undergo a crisis can be found in a recent work by Jean Paul Rosaye's. He asserts that it is possible to document the return to metaphysical speculation in English philosophy throughout the nineteenth century on the grounds of a reassessment that has been taking place in England since the 1980s[20]

The Scottish School

A group of scholars initially gathered in Aberdeen around Thomas Reid, who was its founder and most significant representative, gave raise to the so-called Scottish school, later continued by Dugalt Stewart and Thomas Brown who succeeded him in the chair of moral philosophy in Edinburgh. Although their thought, fundamental to the assimilation of Kantian Criticism in England, led to developments

---

19 Thomas. L.Peacock, *Melincourt.*Complete Novels (London: Rupert Hart Davies, 1963) p. 275 ff. Peacock adumbrated the figure of Coleridge in the grotesque characters of his other satirical novels. Thus he had portrayed him as Mr Panscope in *Headlong Hall.* and will have him dress up as Flosky in *Nightmare Abbey;* in the latter novel the other characters such as Scythrop and Cypress represent Shelley and Byron respectively. Note the explicit irony of some of the names such as Panscope and Cypress alluding the one to the claimed superiority of intuitive knowledge and the sometimes mournful vein of Byron's poetry, the other. Peacock is one of the initiators and major representatives of that literary genre the *novel of talk,* characterised by the tenuousness of the plot and the prominence of the characters skilfully manoeuvred and chastised by satire, which was always good-natured, so that the victims did not usually feel particularly offended.

20 Cfr *F.H. Bradley et l'idealisme britannique.* 2020).

that were beyond the scope of the school's original approach, Hamilton and Mansel can also be considered heirs to this tradition in a certain sense, which they in fact concluded.

For the purposes of our approach, it is necessary to bear in mind above all certain aspects of the theory of knowledge or *gnoseology* (according to the phrasing used at the time) developed by these thinkers, which for a long time were to be the only alternative to the destructive sceptical conclusions of Humean thought. In this sense, this philosophical approach is situated upstream of that revision of classical empiricism which, if on the one hand underpins and substantiates the rebirth and flowering of English idealism, on the other hand, stands, due to its anti-psychologistic critique, as the historical premise of the realist currents that led to the philosophies centered on the of language. It also presents, as has been pointed out by many,[21] significant affinities, albeit only thematic, with Kantian philosophy, insofar as assuming the task of providing a critical response and an alternative to Humean's scepticism, it seeks this response in the identification of the conditions underlying experience. To this affinity, despite its severe limitations, must be ascribed the strong impetus given to the spread and naturalisation of critical philosophy in England, with all the consequences that this dissemination has also entailed for contemporary philosophy.

In a series of works published from 1764 onwards and dedicated to the analysis of the cognitive structure of the human mind, Thomas Reid undertakes, on the basis of the rejection of sceptical elusions, a radical critical revision of empiricism, which takes the form, on a methodological level, of a thorough reconnaissance of the gnoseological theses of Humeans in particular. The purpose of this review is to demonstrate the inconsistency, not so much of inferences and reasoning, but rather of the premises on which the entire Humean analysis rests. I do not intend to examine in detail Reid's criticism, which, apart from being fundamentally outside the scope of my enquiry is marred by simplistic and gross misunderstandings almost all of which can be ascribed to his own difficulty in keeping the theoretical and practical spheres separate.

---

21   Cf. René. Wellek, *Immanuel Kant in England,* 1931)

Instead, it is interesting to note that some concepts that appear in it would later become commonplace in more mature English idealism and would also indirectly influence Russell's philosophy. According to the Scots, Hume's analyses, while constitute a shining example of rigour, lead to erroneous and unacceptable conclusions, and this because they rest on an unexamined and fallacious fundamental assumption that Reid calls 'ideal theory'. The English empiricists are said to have inherited this conception from Descartes. It is the belief that all objects of our knowledge are ideas in our minds. It is precisely this assumption, i.e. the ideal character of knowledge, that constitutes one of the hallmarks of empiricism and prefigures its sceptical conclusion, which Reid considers unjustified because is not supported, in his view, by any evidence. On this objective difficulty inherent in the limited and essentially receptive character of human knowledge, which constitutes one of the most tenacious knots of the entire *gnoseology* Reid imposes, perhaps with excessive nonchalance, his criticism on Hume, so much so as to attract Kant's severe censure.

> Man kan es, ohne eine gewisse Pein zu empfinden, nicht anschen, wie so ganz und gar seine Gegner: Reid, Oswald, Beattie und zuletzt noch Priestley [b]den Punkt seiner Aufgabe verfehlten und, indem sie immer das als zugestanden annahmen, was er eben bezweifelte, dagegen aber mit Heftigkeit und mehrenteils mit großer Unbescheidenheit dasjenige bewiesen was ihm niemals zu bezweifeln in den Sinn gekommen war, seinen Wink zur Verbesserung so verkannten, daßalles in dem alten Zustandeblieb als ob nicht geschehen wäre.[22]

---

22   One cannot look at how his opponents, Reid, Oswald, Beattie, and finally Priestley too, without feeling a certain sense of pity, completely missed the point of the argument: taking for granted what he questioned, and on the contrary vehemently and often arrogantly demonstrating the very thing he had never thought of questioning, they did not understand the signal for reform that he had given, so that everything remained in its old state, as if nothing had happened Immanuel Kant *Prolegomena zu einer jeden künftigen Metaphysik, die als Wissenschaft wird auftreten können*,(F. Meiner Verlag, Hamburg 1951)p. 5[my translation]

Reid and his followers in fact grounded their critique of Humean scepticism by interpreting it not in the sense of a rational, theoretical impossibility of affirming the external, reality of the self and the necessary character of the relations of cause and effect, but as a dogmatic denial of them. The limits of the Reidian reading of Hume[23] should not have escaped Hamilton, however.

The Scottish criticism of scepticism centres on two fundamental theses that Hume admits he is neither able to harmonise nor abandon. The first is the claim that all our distinct perceptions are distinct existences, a thesis that qualifies the fundamental pluralist character of Humean empiricism; the second is that the mind never perceives any real (i.e. necessary) connection between distinct experiences.[24]

Reid rejected both these principles and based his positive alternative on this rejection. Hume himself, moreover, had provided an indication in the quoted passage when he stated that:

> If our perceptions were inherent in something simple and individual or the mind perceived some real connection between them every difficulty would be overcome.[25]

Reid proposed a new theory of knowledge and a new ontology based on an alternative analysis of the constitution of experience that, in his view, overcame scepticism. This analysis resolves itself into a naive realism in which the testimony of the senses is accepted as true on the basis of a belief principle authenticated by common sense (from which the school takes its name), understood

---

23   The *editio princeps* of Reid's works is that of William Hamilton, *The Works of Thomas Reid Now Fully Collected, With Selection: front His Unpublished Letters,* Edinburgh, 1846, accompanied by a very interesting critical apparatus of footnotes which was, however, interrupted due to the death of the editor and later completed by Mansel. This edition was reprinted in 1967 with an introduction by H. M. Bracken by Georg Olms Verlagsbuch-handlung, Hildesheim. Cf. in particular for the purposes of our discussion p. 129 of vol. 1 of this edition.

24   See David. Hume, *A Treatise of Human Nature,* reprinted from the Original Edition in three volumes and edited with an Analytical index by L. A. Selby-Bigge, Oxford, 1888, pp. 634-6.

25   *ibid.*

as the underlying condition of experience.[26] Common sense is, in other words, an ambiguous concept that lies in an unstable balance between the judgement of most and the Kantian a priori, and which nevertheless suffices, according to Reid, to ground the real existence of the subject and the external world.

There is no need to dwell further on the Scotsman's analysis, nor is it necessary to add once again that its founder's tendency to confuse the speculative with the practical aspect of philosophical problems caused him to resoundingly miss the mark in his critique of empiricism.

To limit oneself to this entirely negative balance sheet would, however, be inadequate and unjust because, paradoxically, if the speculative and critical balance sheet of the school taken as a whole cannot be considered positive, it has nonetheless at times made important and fruitful methodological and theoretical contributions. First of all, it should be noted that the school of common sense attempted – first in England – to break with a solid tradition by formulating a critical alternative; in this sense, it is ahead of all subsequent attempts. Moreover, and this specifies and clarifies the meaning of its legacy in the context of the naturalisation of idealist thought in England, because of its afore mentioned thematic affinity with the problematic of criticism, it prepared the ground for the assimilation and development of new modes of thought that would effectively lead to an overcoming of classical empiricism.

---

26   Common sense is understood by Reid as a body of first principles common to all men and, therefore, inescapable. By confusing the theoretical and practical spheres, he frequently tries to show the factual impossibility of living in contravention of those principles and in accordance, instead, with Hume's sceptical conclusions, and then transferring the results of this practical reconnaissance onto the theoretical plane by substantiating them with the notions of general agreement and inescapability. In contrast to Moore, the Reidian notion of a 'common sense' is not the registration of generalised but not therefore theoretically tenable opinions, but rather general principles of knowledge that, however, do not rely on rational demonstrability or self-evidence for their legitimacy, but only on the circumstance of their ascertained or presumed generality. They include contingent truths alongside a priori, mathematical and logical truths. Cf. *Essay on the Intellectual Powers of Man,* Essav VI in Works, cit.

Peculiar to empiricism is a pluralist ontology and gnoseology. That is, the world consists of the sum of particular events and facts. This view implies, on an epistemological level, that knowledge is a sum of particular judgements. Each judgement, is however, a complex composed of the aggregation of individual ideas according to laws. Ideas are thus the true ultimate components and assume in this system the character of epistemological *prius*. It is in this sense that Hume's philosophy acquires the traits of a psychological atomism. The weak point of this gnoseology actually lies in its character as a theory of ideas and in the lack of an adequate theory of their connection into thoughts and expression in judgements. Knowledge, properly meant. in order to be fully configured, necessarily requires the articulation of ideas into thoughts and of judgements into propositions. Now, although Reid cannot be credited with the elaboration of a propositional theory of knowledge, his rejection of atomism and some of his other insights proposes a significant contribution. Despite the fact that his analysis still moves within a psychologistic horizon, it constitutes a step towards the propositional conversion of knowledge that will be fully realised with the subsequent philosophers of language.

We have repeatedly argued that a common feature at the heart of Russellian thought is the separation of logical analysis from psychological analysis and the assumption of judgement and proposition as the starting point for the analysis of knowledge, rather than the idea or concept. The propositional conversion of knowledge is the end point of a critique of empiricism that the Scottish school, regardless of its theoretical limitations, has effectively set up. This critique reveals a design that unfolds along three main lines: firstly: the critique of the empiricist concept of idea; secondly: the thesis of the propositionality of perception, i.e. the implication of a judgement in every perception; and thirdly: the consequent thesis that judgement, i.e. the complex, precedes analysis, which amounts to the refutation of the atomistic character of knowledge. Reid seems to be the first to elaborate a critique of the empiricist concept of idea that, by varying its traits, will be taken up by both Bradley and Russell. He states that, as used by the empiricists in general and by Hume in particular, the view that the notion of of idea is the vehicle of an irredeemaable ambiguity and generates misunderstandings that transcend the purely terminological sphere, affecting the entire theory of knowledge. In his view,

> Locke sometimes confuses ideas with the perception of an external object, sometimes with the external object itself. In Berkeley's system the idea is the only object and yet it is often confused with the perception of it. But in Hume's system the idea or impression, which is only a more vivid idea, is at once the spirit, the perception, and the object; so that by the term perception in Hume's system we must mean the mind, all its operations both of intellection and of will, and all the objects of these operations.[27]

In short, Reid noted, without succeeding in taking it to extreme consequences, that classical empiricism did not allow for a distinction between the different meanings of ideas, thus leading to a conception of knowledge that accredits the representational content of ideas with structural interconnection capacities that it cannot adequately justify, while recourse to the mechanisms of association or to vague and ambiguous concepts such as those of the greater and lesser force of images not being based on the representational content – the only one that, in the Humean system, legitimately sustains differences – seems inadequate and insufficient.

The Philosophy of the Absolute: F. H. Bradley

The critique of the ambiguity of the concept of the idea is of great importance; it conveyed directly or indirectly and, one might say, in spite of the positive doctrine of the Scottish school, an important and radical revision of classical empiricism and in particular the overcoming of the psychologistic vocation that also represents its limit. Let us now try to trace, albeit roughly, the route followed by this critique. Reid, as we have seen, pointed out the ambiguities inherent in the failure to distinguish between the activity of the spirit, the

---

27   Cf. Reid, *Inquiry into the Human Mind, in Works* pp. 182 ff. *Essays on the Intellectual Powers of Man,* II ch. IX p. 279 and ch. XII, p. 294; see also D. Hume, *Treatise,* cit., book I, part III sec. VII, pp. 96-7 (footnote).

psychological image and the object or content of this image.[28] The Humean system, taking Locke's 'new way of ideas' to extremes, did not allow a way out of the internal spectacle and Reid's evasion runs on the insecure ground of naive common sense dogmatism. Reid's precise and articulate distinction between perception and sensation[29], although like all his analysis moves on a stubbornly psychologistic horizon, structurally prefigures the analyses that will lead realists and idealists out of the shallows of psychologism.

> When we consider sensation in itself,' says Bradley, 'and separate it from the other things united to it in the imagination, it becomes clear that it is something that cannot exist except in a sentient spirit and cannot be distinguished from the act of the mind that feels it: whereas perception always has an object distinct from the act of perceiving. When I smell a rose, that is, perception and sensation are united in that operation. The smell considered in itself beyond a relation to the rose is the sensation. Perception, on the other hand, has an external object – the rose's quality of emitting the scent – and the act of my spirit attests to that quality and perception.[30]

In terms of the philosophy of language, Reid's analysis sets, if not the contents, certainly the structure of a theory of reference and meaning that, transferred from the psychological to the logical level and above all articulated in a theory of judgement, will substantiate the propositional vocation of subsequent philosophy, that is to say, what will be called the – Revolution in Philosophy.[31] In a broader

---

28 It should be noted, *passim*, that this tripartition obscurely anticipates the one that Brentano advances in his *Psychologie vom Empirischen Standpunkt.*

29 See Reid, *Essays on the Intellectual Powers of Man,* part II ch. I and *Inquiry into the Human Mind,* ch. II sec. VII, p. 110, in *Works*

30 Cf. F. H. Bradley, *Principles of Logic,* p. 329

31 As a matter of fact fact, Reid agrees with Moore and Russell in the view that language is a guide to ontology. This will be one of the fundamental theses of Russell who will argue that "the study of grammar can throw light on philosophical questions". Indeed, Reid holds that all perception implies judgement, i.e. in more contemporary terms, he affirms the propositional character of knowledge, or at least implies it. On this very important point for its development in contemporary thought see Reid,

and different framework, that is to say, in the framework of a definition of the nature of philosophy that, due to the peculiarity of his thought, he will carry out in a critical and negative form, Bradley returns to the analysis of the idea as a unit of knowledge and will make this analysis one of the cornerstones of his anti-empirical polemic. Bradley will first of all reject the *view* according to which philosophy is the study of thought and knowledge as it is shown through the examination of images and perceptions. In other words, he places himself at the antipodes of that physiology of perception, of that genetic reconstruction of representations in which the "plain historical method" is configured, and with which Locke wanted to investigate the constitution of knowledge through the examination of the functions of the different faculties of the human spirit. It is thus precisely because of his rejection of this psychologistic vocation that Bradley will, as we shall see later, re-approach the analysis of the concept of the idea, the results of which are of considerable importance in the development of Russell's philosophy. When Russell sets out on his initial reconstruction of empiricism he would thus have behind him a fairly well-established tradition of revision, many elements of which would flow directly into his thought; and first and foremost the clear separation of psychology and philosophy that is a direct consequence of the results of Bradley's analysis of the concept of idea.

The pluralist horizon of Russell's philosophy is not, therefore, a component directly and solely inherited from the empiricist tradition, but the result of a recovery and renewal of it that passes through the refutation of the monist neo-Hegelianism then in vogue and the preparation of new methodological tools. A number of factors contributed to Russell's radical and definitive detachment from monism, including the realisation of the impossibility of mathematics within monism, the influence of Moore on his thinking and, above all, the development of the theory of external relations.

Essays on the Intellectual Powers of Man, p. 327 and Bracken's preface to the collection of works. See also J. H. Jacques, 'The Appeal to Common Sense' pp. 709-10; 715.

The most mature and significant expression of Bradley's thought is to be found in *Appearance and Reality.* It is a rather complex thought [32] expressed in language that is more suggestive than rigorous, in which polemical impetus and general critical inspiration predominate decisively over positive doctrine.[33] Such a configuration can be explained, at least in part, by bearing in mind the polemical intentions and reaction to the theory of knowledge of Stuart-Mill and of all empiricism in general to which his philosophy responded.

The fundamental thesis of Bradleyan idealism is ontological monism. Reality is an indivisible unity that he calls the Absolute. The multiplicity witnessed by the senses is, instead, pure appearance and in any case a reflex of our inability to grasp reality itself. The plurality of events, objects and persons and the relations between the different elements of this multiplicity is completely illusory.

This doctrine, however, is not the result of an investigation pursued with the methods of empirical knowledge. Rather, it is the result of an abstract speculation that supports the unreality of multiplicity on the basis of a judgement of its self-contradictory nature.[34] The logic underlying Bradley's ontology is actually closer to Parmenides than to Hegel.[35] But the most singular and in some ways self-destructive aspect of Bradley's monism is his belief in the incommensurability of thought to Reality, that is, to the absolute. The absolute cannot be grasped in thought because thought is relational and moves from fact to fact, from term to term and is therefore irreparably bound to a pluralist vision; its field is therefore necessarily that of appearance. If both, the senses and thought draw nothing but appearances, the

---

32   There have been also those who argued polemically that "it would be very difficult to say what exactly his philosophy was, if anything at all." See Geoffrey J. Warnock, *English Philosophy Since* 1900, Oxford, 1969, p. 2.

33   Bradley's renunciation of a systematic structure has, as we have seen, a theoretical root in the thesis of the incommensurability of reality to thought. See footnote 8.

34   Contradiction, as we have seen, is not in Bradley – unlike in Hegel – the way in which reality is constituted and thought; rather, it is conceived as a sign of the illusory nature of appearance.

35   See John Passmore, *A Hundred Years of Philosophy,* p. 60.

question remains as to what this absolute is and of which appearances are just such.

Bradley's puzzling answer[36] is that Reality is its appearances'. The relationship between appearances and Reality could be likened to that between the limbs and the body to which they belong or between the ingredients of a mixture and the mixture. But these analogies are only partially satisfactory. While the former, highlighting the conditional character of the existence of appearances with respect to Reality, attributes to them a partially autonomous statute of existence, the latter sins in the opposite sense by accentuating the radical and intrinsic change that the part undergoes in the whole so that two distinct moments in the life of the part are given: before and after integration into the absolute; and the result is to give inadequate prominence to the moment of difference. According to Bradley, on the other hand, they really are what they are, that is, they are themselves only in the absolute; and there is no doubt that the concept is obscure and difficult to interpret. A more satisfactory analogy might be that which likens the Bradleyan absolute to a work of art, for example to a painting.[37] The relationship between appearances and Reality would be overshadowed. in this case, by that between the details of the work and the work as a whole. In this way, the conflicting demands of the autonomy of the parts and the unity of the work are safeguarded, in the sense that the detail. while always remaining as such in the whole, nevertheless acquires its true and full meaning only in the whole. The consequences of this philosophy are numerous and complex. We will only dwell on those that most directly affect the relationship with Russell's philosophy.

Firstly, the statement of Reality as an organic whole implies the denial of the separate and independent existence of the external world whose apparent multiplicity and independence is only to be attributed to our inability to grasp the Absolute. In short, the distinction between a knowing subject and the known object falls away. The perception of a single fact or object – upon which all empiricist epistemology is based – is flawed according to Bradley

---

36   Cf. *Appearance and Reality,* ch. 24.
37   See R. Wollheim, *F.H.Bradley,*pp. 226-7.

in the sense that it is an abstraction and a privileging of one part of experience. Our fragmentary knowledge, by not grasping the entire network of connections that connects the single experience to the others and gradually to the Whole, mutilates Reality rather than grasping it and therefore has no authentic cognitive value since the partial element acquires, as we have seen, its meaning only in integration with all the others. The propositions in which empirical knowledge is configured, i.e. the particular judgements, are therefore irretrievably false. The only truth being the proposition that attributes a predicate to the absolute. But even this truth cannot ultimately be affirmed on pain of mutilation and self-contradiction since the attribution of a universal predicate to the one Reality still entails the distinction of the Subject of the predicate and thus contradicts the unity of the Whole.

At the end of 1898, after having more than adhered to it for a few years, Russell abandoned Bradley's doctrine and reaffirmed the fundamental pluralist instance, laying the foundations of that reconstruction of empiricism that through its attempt at a logical reconstruction of knowledge would culminate in the *Philosophy of Logical Atomism.*

The rejection and refutation of monist ontology and the transition to pluralism will rest, above all, on the elaboration of that theory of 'external relations' that is one of the fundamental philosophical acquisitions of the early Russell, bound to play a fundamental role in the further developments of his thought. The theory of external relations exemplifies, on the other hand, the first application of logical analysis to general philosophical problems and plainly illustrates, as we shall see, the way in which notions such as those of 'logical form', 'reference' and 'isomorphism' operate in Russell's philosophy, endowing analytical practice with authentic philosophical values.

CHAPTER TWO
A NEGLECTED LEGACY

An attempt at a reconstruction, or: empiricism revisited

Russell's philosophy exhibits, as a whole, a structure rooted in the articulation of a logical and a gnoseological component. It represents an attempt, only partially successful, to clothe and exemplify a logical structure, assumed to be metaphysically neutral, with a theory of knowledge of an empirical approach. It is precisely this second component and the attempt to weld it with logical theory that will be at the origin of various difficulties of Russellian atomism and will result in a metaphysics that will be interpreted as a sort of diffracted image of idealist metaphysics.[1] It will be precisely the search for the empirical exemplification of analytical residues that will determine the differences between Russellian atomism and that of the early Wittgenstein.

The logical structure is fundamentally made up of the theory of representation and structural isomorphism between language and the world and by the thesis of the reciprocal logical (and ontological) independence of the components of propositions and facts, as also appears in Wittgenstein's *Tractatus*. Russell then makes an attempt to weld with the empiricist theory of knowledge insofar as, unlike Wittgenstein, he seeks to identify the ultimate components of analysis with the elementary perceptual units of empiricist theory of knowledge: sensory data. The very general assumption of isomorphism between language and facts grounds, therefore, the main theoretical underpinning of all Russellian metaphysics and, in particular, of the philosophy of logical atomism. It is articulated in

---

1   Cf. John Passmore, *Russell and Bradley* pp. 21-30.

two distinct moments that, together, contribute to determining its philosophical value: the notion of *logical form* and the referential theory of meaning. Two components that represent, respectively, the syntactic and semantic aspects of Russell's analysis of language, so that if on the one hand the analysis of form is an investigation of the way in which the components of reality, linguistic and otherwise, are articulated and structured, the investigation of meanings goes beyond or matches the structural moment to provide an ontological vision of the ultimate components of the world. We will return to the relationship between language and extra-linguistic reality several times in the following pages; here it is important above all to clarify, in general terms and for introductory purposes only, the concept of logical form since it underlies Russell's first important theoretical acquisition; the re-foundation of pluralist ontology which, with the overcoming of monist idealism, marks the beginning of a reconstruction of empiricism in which all of Russell's thought is embedded.

The form of a proposition is, according to Russell, the structure of the articulation of its components considered independently of them; the pure pattern underlying the specific content, the way, that is, in which the parts are linked together. Propositions such as "Socrates is mortal"; "the sky is blue" or "Charles is jealous", although deal with evidently different contents, have the same structure which, in this case, is exhibited by the predicative use of the verb common to all three. Each one, in fact, can be obtained from the other by transformation, replacing the components of one with those of the other. In other cases one can, conversely, have propositions of different forms with the same components as in "Socrates was an Athenian" and "Socrates died drinking hemlock". Since it is possible to obtain propositions with different contents but the same form, it follows from this that the form is not an additional component of the propositions.

It is easy to understand how the metaphysical presupposition of isomorphism implies that the analysis of the form of propositions does not constitute an activity aimed at the mere exhibition of the syntactic features of our language or, perhaps more correctly, of our historically given language and, therefore, at a deeper knowledge of it, but is, above all, specified as an exquisitely philosophical activity. The correct explication of the formal structure of propositions is, in effect, the instrument for exhibiting the structure of the facts that correspond to them. This analysis, which Russell includes as part of logic, has the task of "extracting this knowledge from its concrete covers and making it explicit and pure"[2]. It is within this framework that the thesis that the failure to recognise the importance of the investigation of form has had major metaphysical consequences is placed. Indeed, he argues that

> the influence of language on philosophy has, I believe, been profound and almost unrecognized. – and that – if we are not to be misled by this influence, it is necessary to become conscious of it and to ask ourselves deliberately how far it is legitimate. The subject-predicate logic with the substance-attribute metaphysics, are a case in point.[3]

Since almost all propositions can be expressed or constructed in a subject-predicate form, it was inferred, Russell argued, from this linguistic form the form of the real, that is, affirming the metaphysical doctrine that every fact is constituted by a substance that possesses a quality, and this metaphysics of substance was to ground, as we shall see, monism.

Syntax is not, however, the only aspect of language to be taken into account. A further deepening of the level of analysis is that which investigates the consistency of those concrete 'covers' of propositions that are words. Lexicon, in short, is also of considerable philosophical importance. If the formal structure of propositions reflects the configurations of facts, words are responsible for our beliefs about their components and, consequently, the components of the world. We thus reach the second moment of Russell's philosophical grammar.

Alongside the notion of logical form, or rather within it, a referential theory of meaning acts in Russellian philosophy. The meaning of

---

2   Bertrand Russell, *Our Knowledge of the External World*) p. 53
3   Bertrand Russell, *Logical Atomism* in J.Muirhead (ed.), *Contemporary British Philosophy,* rpr. in R. C. Marsh ((ed.) *Logic and Knowledge, essays* 1901-1950 (London, George Allen& Unwin, 1956) p. 330

linguistic expressions is, according to this theory, identified with the things that the expressions themselves designate and refer to.

The condition for a word to have meaning is that there be the 'thing' it designates, that is, that a *denotatum* be given that constitutes the ontological correlate of linguistic expressions. It is easy to see how the referential theory of meaning thus operates the welding of the two planes: logical and ontological. Every element of language must in fact correspond to some extra-linguistic real entity in the world, on pain of the insignificance of symbolism.

This correspondence between proposition and fact, between elements of the proposition and elements of the facts, is the structure that facts and propositions share, namely that logical form that constitutes the object of investigation of linguistic analysis. And it is this structural identity or isomorphism between propositions and facts that makes linguistic analysis a genuinely philosophical enterprise. Indeed, on the one hand, it is a tool for explicating the functioning of symbolism and thus leading to a more correct use of language, but at the same time, the assumption of structural isomorphism makes it a method of investigating reality.

Such a concise schematisation of the analytical method might, however, erroneously suggest that a scrupulous surveillance of our language and an inspection of the forms of propositions are the easy tools for the investigation of reality; in fact, the fundamental structure of facts and propositions is not so easily displayed: Ordinary language, rather than exhibiting the fundamental structure of facts and propositions, conceals it behind grammatical form, and many expressions that appear, at first sight, to designate real entities have, on the contrary, no ontological counterpart and, therefore, are not meaningful even if they appear to be so. Logical analysis operates. therefore, by means of techniques aimed at exhibiting the true logical structure of propositions so as to reveal their true form and to restructure them in such a way that they appear as composed only of truly denoting expressions. This reconstruction is the method of philosophical investigation and makes use of analytical techniques that Russell mostly borrowed from the methodology of logic and mathematics.

The entire programme tends, ideally, towards the construction of a perfect, totally transparent language, in which the logical form appears, immediately evident. It is a philosophical enterprise that substantiates an ambitious attempt to reconstruct empiricism on a logical basis that can be considered the core and the goal of his philosophy.

This brief mention is only a prerequisite to understand in which problem horizon and methodological context is rooted that new interpretation of relations that is the most relevant philosophical acquisition of Russell's first production and that will allow the setting of the pluralist instance against Bradley's idealist monism.

On the overcoming and refutation of monism rests, in fact, all the subsequent developments of his research and, above all, logical constructionism and atomism. The doctrine of relations underlying Russellian pluralism is not only one of the fundamental issues of the revolutionary reduction of mathematics to logic offered in *Principia Mathematica,* but also the focal point of a dispute addressed against the English idealist tradition.

In April 1899, the appearance of an article[4] by the then 25-year-old Moore virtually marked the end of the English idealist school; but perhaps it would be more accurate to say the beginning of that frontal attack later continued also by Russell, which would lead to its overcoming, marking at the same time a fundamental turning point in contemporary, not only, Anglo-Saxon thought. In reality, then, even though its theoretical foundations had by then been refuted, the idealist school was still to give indirect proof of its hold on culture and, above all, on English universities if in 1924, and in the following year when the *Tractatus* and *Principia Mathematica* had already been published, were to see the light of day two volumes with a clearly idealist slant, bearing the anachronistic title of *Contemporary British Philosophy*[5].

---

4   *The Nature of judgement* published in *Mind,* followed in 1903 by the fundamental *Refutation of Idealism,* also published in *Mind.* For an evaluation of the importance of Moore's contribution, see the already cited Ayer, *Russell and Moore*

5   The collection, including essays by various authors, is preceded by an introduction by Muirhead in which, with inexplicable prejudice against the radical changes in perspective and method that had taken place in

They represented rather a retrospective than a contemporary overview. The turning point in Anglo-Saxon philosophical thought, indeed, was so radical as to make the systematic claims of the idealist school definitively outdated and unfit to stimulate contemporary consciousness. Bradley and McTaggart appeared as far and apart from Russell and Moore as the pre-Socratics might have been from Descartes. We will try in the following to show how this appearance did not correspond so much to reality.

As was been observed, British neo-Hegelianism did not die of refutation, but rather of self-exhaustion[6], and the consciousness of the profoundly innovative and revolutionary character of the new philosophy became so deeply ingrained in the new thinkers that they did not for many years give serious consideration to the real relationship between the old and the new philosophy. Against this backdrop, a view of contemporary Anglo-Saxon thought matured as completely isolated from its immediate predecessors and, if anything, reconnected in a certain way to the classical empiricist tradition. This is only partly true, and access to hitherto unknown documents supported since then the effort for a necessary historical re-examination of the network of mutual theoretical relationships. In March 1968, about two years before his death, Russell gave his library and all his personal papers – a gigantic archive inventoried in a 343-page volume covering most but not all of it – to McMaster University in Hamilton, Canada. After a year spent sorting, placing and reducing *this material* to microfilm, the archives were opened to the public with extreme liberality and with the only restrictions imposed by copyright and by the constraints placed on private correspondence with people still living; a periodical entitled *Russell was* also published, since then with the aim of making available to the scolars the contents of the archives and acting as a

---

philosophical research, he supported the view that English philosophy had become part of the continental tradition, also expressing the hope that the younger generations of philosophers (of which Russell and Moore were part) would continue to flourish there (!)

6   See G.J. Warnock, p. 7. According to Warnock, metaphysical systems are not susceptible to frontal attacks because they are characterised by the singular property of being demonstrable only from within; a circumstance that makes them impregnable from without.

clearing house for Russell studies. The archives have also set out to acquire, through purchase, exchange and donations from public bodies and private individuals, further material; and indeed the archive was since then to grow continuously. The most important of these further acquisitions is what passes for the 'second Russell archive', consisting of material that Russell did not initially wish to hand over, namely letters written on behalf of the Bertrand Russell Peace Foundation and letters 'which are confidential' in addition to the considerable material that accumulated in the four years between the sale of the first archive and Russell's death, totalling some 75,000 items. The opening of the Russell archives has been undoubtedly an event destined, in time, to shed new light on the personality and thought of the English philosopher and in many cases to rectify the image that has been given, especially concerning his relations with the culture of his time. In fact, the archives are in possession not only of an immense private correspondence (thousands and thousands of letters) exchanged by Russell with major contemporary thinkers (Bradley, Meinong, Wittgenstein, Whitehead, Moore to name but a few philosophers) of interest that is far from being limited to the biographical aspect and that indeed testifies to the itinerary and development of his thinking and has already proved indispensable for a correct understanding of his work, also a very significant number of unpublished and original alternative versions of writings that were later published and that began to offer the materials for a promising reconstruction that was to prove anything but significant surprises. There were unpublished manuscripts on the concept of material implication, on denotation and the notion of truth, the 1913 typescript of a book on the theory of knowledge not published due to Wittgenstein's criticism, to name but a few examples. A material, in short, that in quantity and quality is very interesting and to which many scholars were profitably to direct their enquiries.The Journal *RUSSELL* was founded by the McMaster University Library in 1971.[7].

---

7   In the summer of 1981 began a new series. Since 1971 Russell has been dedicated to the study of all aspects of Bertrand Russell's thought, as well as his life, times and influence. For the first 51 years of publication, Russell was edited by Kenneth Blackwell. Andrew Bone and Gülberk Koç Maclean have been the editors since 2022.

Russell's philosophy certainly represented an evolution and a development of the empiricist tradition; a continuation in the sense that between Humean pluralism and Russellian atomism there is no theoretical break but mainly an evolutionary continuity and a growth.

The analysis of experience underlying Russell's theory of knowledge, although falling *de facto* and *de jure* within the sphere of empiricist reductionism, achieved far more relevant and sophisticated results than those reached by the classical empiricists; and this thanks to the possibilities offered by a more rigorous and sophisticated conceptual and logical apparatus. Russellian atomism goes beyond the limits of Hume's because it transcends the psychologistic approach implicit in the analysis of experience grounded in the analysis of mental states, and replaces the analysis of ideas seen as psychic entities with the analysis of the propositions and the judgements in which thought is expressed.

Russell's atomism, like Hume's, is grounded on a pluralist worldview, in which reality consists of a multiplicity of mutually independent entities; and it is this that legitimises analysis as a philosophical practice aimed at reduction of complexes to their constituent elements; but whereas the classical empiricists worked on ideas by reducing the complex to the simple and moved on a topics that today forms the subject of investigations of empirical psychology, the modern atomists turned to logical analysis, changing the 'new way of ideas' into a new way of words. The ontological relevance of this analysis is linked however to the acceptance of a non-empirical assumption which is the structural identity between logic and extralinguistic reality.

This assumption, which goes hand in hand with the postulation of simple elements, i.e. with the establishment of a necessary stopping point for analysis, has enabled the reduction of the multiplicity of the real to its supposed constituent elements through the reduction of the complexity of language to elementary or atomic propositions and, of the latter, to their constituent elements and the consequent postulate

---

Beginning with the Summer 2023 issue the journal is published in print and digital format by Johns Hopkins University Press *RUSSELL* continues to be produced by the Bertrand Russell Research Centre in McMaster.

of the isomorphic, structural correlation of the residues of the two streams of analysis.

It was a programme grounded not only on the metaphysical assumption of structural isomorphism and the postulation of simple entities, but also on an extensional conception of language and truth, in turn, grounded on the of the mutual logical independence of propositions.

The difficulties that would stand in the way of the execution of this ambitious analytical programme would be numerous and sometimes so radical as to lead to a rapid attrition of the theory, even if the methodological instance it embodies would be preserved. It is worth noting the significant analogy of this position with Hume's doctrine of the mutual independence of perceptions. The *truth-functional* theory of language and truth (according to which the truth or falsity of complex propositions is a function of the truth or falsity of atomic propositions) represents the logico-linguistic version of the empiricist theory that wants complex ideas to be functions of the aggregation of simple ones.

Beyond and irrespective of the innovative character of logical atomism, it is clear that the links with the empiricist tradition go far beyond a general common approach. The debt to classical empiricism has, however, been widely recognised and directly acknowledged by Russell himself, who often explicitly referred to this tradition. The assumption, on the other hand, of idealism as a mere polemical target has somehow underestimated if not passed over in silence a positive legacy that Bradley, at least, left, especially with his *Logic* to the thinkers who succeeded him. If we disregard, and for our purposes it is necessary to do so, an overall evaluation, Bradley's thought seems worth placing not in the museum of a paleo-philosophy in which the developments of the new pluralistic realism have, in the beginning in fact placed him, but rather in that intermediate zone that marks the border between a preminently metaphysical and systematic philosophy and the analytical-linguistic "turn" that characterised further philosophical thought. Bradley's logic has the merit, not universally recognised or at least not sufficiently noted, of having initiated that critique of classical logic that, through the contributions of Frege and Peano, would culminate in the *Principia Mathematica.*

Traditional propositional analysis had in Bradley a critic as severe as the exponents of the symbolic logic. Like Frege, and independently of him, he drew attention to the fact that the grammatical form of utterances can conceal, rather than reveal, the logical form. What differentiates him from philosophers that came after him and embeds his thought in its time is the relationship between his logic and his metaphysics. The discovery of the insufficiency of syllogistic logic, the ambiguities of grammatical forms, in short, the insufficiency of the traditional analysis of the proposition do not serve Bradley as starting points for an alternative investigation of reality and language; he does not aim at replacing new propositional forms for the old, but only to show the incommensurability of thought and language with respect to reality.

The detection and accentuation of the artificiality, universality and designative inability of language are as many merely critical platforms with which to condemn as an appearance, not true, all human knowledge that is not knowledge of the whole, of the absolute. But this critical limit and the subsidiary office towards metaphysics to which Bradley bends his logic and the purely negative dimension do not detract from the sharpness of some of his analyses which not only exerted a definite influence but, integrated in a different conceptual apparatus, reappeared with much greater force, scope and effectiveness in the thought of Russell and his successors. The polemical and metaphysical context has, on the other hand, provided a convenient alibi and a curtain that has allowed many critics to ignore the most vital aspects of his thought, so that the links that generally connect the most mature English idealism to those streams committed to a revision in a logical sense of empiricism have been, in fact, concealed and consequently the controversy between Russell and Bradley has been reduced to the dimensions of a clash of two heterogeneous and irreconcilable thinkers.

Many enquiries on Russell's thought dwell only briefly on the youthful transition from idealistic monism to pluralism and the controversy with Bradley that engaged the two thinkers for some thirty years. This is, however, a significant and suggestive period, the in-depth study of which allows to review schematic judgements on English idealism and the general cultural function it exercised.

It is precisely from the refutation of Hegelism, at first accepted, that Russell's true philosophical personality took shape, the further developments of which lead, as we have said, to a recovery of those pluralist and realist instances that are part of the classical English tradition. Russell's contribution to contemporary thought is, on the whole, precisely an attempt at a radical renewal of that tradition routed in the application to classical doctrine of far more effective methodological tools of analysis. The pursuit of a scientific methodology of philosophizing through the use of logic to traditional philosophical problems and the elaboration of logical atomism are then connected, both methodologically and theoretically, to the genesis and development of those analytical methods, irreducible by definition to a systematic philosophy, characterised by the rejection of metaphysics (a rejection that does not directly concern Russell) and of the speculative method of investigation on the one hand, and by the priority given to the analysis of language as method and function of philosophy on the other.

The change of perspective with respect to the previous philosophical tradition was so radical and so deeply felt as to be described in terms of a "turning point" or "revolution", so that, while the generally innovative character and characterising thematic elements stood out clearly, it also endorsed the image of a theoretical and methodological independence and autonomy that was certainly superior to reality. English idealist philosophy in general and Bradley's in particular, acquired in this framework the role of a mere polemical target or theoretical antagonist whose contribution to contemporary thought would be all and only negative, in the sense that its only function would be to be refuted and supplanted.

This season of English philosophy appears as a very significant parenthesis in Anglo-Saxon culture and should not be reduced to a mere importation of foreign problems and motifs.[8] The thesis of the impossibility of grasping the meaning of Russell's philosophy

---

8   On the peculiar character and developments of idealist thought in England see Muirhead, *The Platonic Tradition in Anglo saxon Philosophy,* London, 1931); Jean Pucelle, *L'idealisme en Angleterre,* de *Coleridge a Bradle* (Neuchatel:1955; Francois Houang, *Le neohegelianisme en Angleterre* (Paris: Vrin, 1954).

outside of an investigation that historicizes it, placing it in the context of the reaction to English idealism and thus linking it above all to Bradley, who in turn would be almost unintelligible unless the eminently critical structure of his thought were interpreted within the reaction to empiricist gnoseology, and in particular that of Stuart Mill, has already been put forward in a now classic study on the origins of analytic philosophy in England.[9]

This need for historicization, which generally only expresses a correct habit of enquiry, implies, in Russell's case, some specific problems from which lively polemics were nourished. In fact, his work as the initiator of the "linguistic turn" and thus of a true revolution in philosophical enquiry is conceived has made him share the fate of the initiators, that is, it has made him the subject of a revolt against his own father by the followers and proponents of analytic philosophy, who have quickly relegated him in the mausoleum of illustrious but hopelessly outdated ancestors whose teaching has been necessary to both learn and overcome. On the other hand, the innovative nature of his problematics and methodology has very often led to an overestimation of originality in his thought, thus spreading a tenacious curtain over the links that connect him, albeit problematically and sometimes polemically with the historical context and tradition in which he matured.

Awareness of the profoundly innovative and revolutionary character of the philosophy inspired by the 'new way of words' has, however, taken root so quickly that it has not allowed, if not prevented even for many years, a proper examination of the exact determination of the relationship between the old and the new philosophy.

Instead, a view of Russell's thought as wholly or fundamentally independent of its immediate idealist predecessors and, if anything, directly connected to the classical tradition of empiricism and Hume in particular, has matured, or rather spread rather uncritically.[10]

---

9   J. O. Urmson, *Philosophical Analysis*, pp. 14 ff.
10   For a well-known example of this interpretation of Russell's philosophy see David.F. Pears, *Bertrand Russell and the British Tradition in Philosophy* (London: Collins,1968); as well as the already cited Ayér, *Russell and Moore: The Analytical Heritage.*

It is within this framework that the dispute, or rather the reconstruction of the controversy has pitted Bradley and Russell against each other for many years as champions of irreconcilably opposed and, above all, absolutely unrelated and uncommunicative philosophies and methodologies.

The view of total extraneousness and with it the reduction of the complex web of relations to a question of frontal opposition does not actually account for the richness of the issue at hand. The picture is far more articulated than the theory of frontal opposition lets on. Alongside the real logical-metaphysical dispute between monism and pluralism, there are significant points of convergence that a hasty assessment has too quickly buried.

Russell's philosophy represents, in fact, an only partially successful attempt to renew the empiricist tradition and its reframing in a logical-analytical key, an attempt that passes through the polemic and refutation of Bradley's idealistic monism that would represent a temporary interruption of the tradition.

The lesson of the relationship between Bradley and Russell or, if you like, between English neo-idealist philosophy and analytic philosophy in terms of pure opposition is, even if accredited, excessively reductive; it sins at least in Manichaeism and, above all. seems to be founded on the identification of the whole Bradley's thought with a single work: *Appearance and Reality* which, although it represents the most mature expression of his metaphysics of the absolute, certainly does not exhaust his contribution. Of course, it is not intended here to dispute that the empiricist component is the one that best qualifies Russell's thought; What we wish to state firstly is that the recovery of the interrupted empiricist tradition did not take place in Russell directly, i.e. by skipping the idealist phase of English thought and, secondly, that Bradley's philosophy did not represent in the framework of Russell's theoretical maturation only a negative moment whose overcoming lies at the basis of further analytical outcomes. It exercised, in reality, a definite positive influence even if little recognised. While the debt to classical empiricism has been widely acknowledged and recalled not only by the critics but also by Russell himself, English idealist philosophy in general and Bradley's thought in particular seem to have been hastily characterised in the critical literature with a more or less direct adherence to Russell's viewpoint,[11] thus obscuring, by identifying Bradley's work with only his *Appearance and Reality* alone, a positive contribution traceable above all in the *Logic,* which was to exercise, as we will try to document, a precise positive function in the development of Russell's more mature thought.

On the one hand, this is not surprising; the usual generosity and balance with which Russell usually acknowledged and testified to his intellectual debts is strangely lacking in Bradley's case. Although he studied and annotated his *Logic* at an early age, he identified the idealist philosopher with the metaphysician, the author of *Appearance and Reality,* with the supporter of the doctrine of internal relations, a doctrine that he considered the logical scaffolding of monism. Russell quoted Bradley many times, but almost always to refute his theory of relations. Only in two cases the polemic has been accompanied by momentarily giving way to an albeit vague acknowledgement of some intellectual debt.[12] It is not surprising, then, that the critical literature has mostly embraced an essentially negative assessment of Bradley's work and the *tout court* identification of his work with *Appearance and Reality.*

On the one hand, therefore, Russell's overwhelming philosophical personality acted as a hindrance to an independent reconnaissance of

---

11   Which appears, above all, in his versions of the relations with idealist monism that Russell himself delivered in his two intellectual autobiographies

12   Cf. T*he Philosophy of Leibniz*, pp. 12-15 and p.44-45;177.; *The Principles of mathematics,* p.221 ch. XXVI on relations in which he criticises the Bradleyan argument against relations based on an alleged regress to infinity; *Our knowledge of the External world,* pp.16; 47-8; 169-70. *Analysis of Mind* p. 468???. The only quotations in which he even vaguely acknowledges a debt to Bradley are to be found in *Principles of Mathematics* in the chapter on Implication, "The Philosophy of Logical Atomism" in *Logic and Knowledge,* in which he acknowledges Bradley as the author of the thesis according to which universal statements are hypothetical and not categorical and "Logical Atomism", p. 324; for a synthetic attempt at an overall evaluation of the influence exerted by Bradley on B. Russell's philosophical thought see C. N. Keen, 'The Interaction of Russell and Bradley' in *Russell,* III, (1971), p. 7-11.13

Bradley's work, and on the other hand, the published texts support this thesis but are insufficient for a reconstruction and recomposition of the picture of the relationships between the two philosophers. The opening of the Russell archives and the publication of its contents, including a private correspondence between the two philosophers over a period of about 22 years, have since then made possible to shed a clearer light on these relations and, above all, have provided, rather than irrefutable proof, the suggestion and direction for further research aimed at correctly assessing – beyond diaristic versions on the integral reliability of which it is legitimate to advance some doubts – the positive role played by Bradley's work in the formation of his thought.[13]

Beyond the uncertain category of influence, which is always rather equivocal, some characteristic issues of Russellian reflection seem to be traceable, with the support of precise references to Bradley's work. The issues to which we refer are inscribed in that anti-psychological critique from which Bradley's corrosive philosophy took its cue and anticipate the developments of that philosophy that places at the centre of reflection the language of which Russell was, perhaps wrongly, considered the sole initiator, at least in England.

---

13   The correspondence held in the Russell Archives consists of 23 letters sent by Bradley to Russell between 1901 and 1914 and 11 letters sent by Russell to Bradley covering a period of time from 1900 to 1922. Other documents in the archive show that Russell first read, and minutely annotated, Bradley's *Logic* in 1893, *Ethical Studies* in May 1894 and *Appearance and Reality* in August of the same year. It is quite remarkable that a private correspondence marked by expressions of undoubted esteem is matched by Russell's total silence in his published writings. When Russell met Bradley for the first time in December 1902, he noted in his diary that he 'felt a deep affection for the man' and in a letter to him in 1907 he wrote: 'Let me tell you that I have learned more from his works than from those of any other philosopher of our time, and that in ceasing to agree with his system I have not lost the slightest part of the high respect which I have always felt for his thought'. quoted by Jack Pitt in 'With Russell at the Archives' *Russell,* The Journal of the Bertrand Russell Archives (1971), p. 4.

We will try to discuss some of these issues separately[14] sometimes showing their Bradleyan genesis with *ad hoc* references.

Anti-psychological prodromes

Although the distinction between psychology investigation and philosophy appears today clearly defined, nonetheless it matured only very gradually between the end of nineteenth and twentieth century and has entailed the laborious overcoming of a conception of the tasks of philosophy that dates back at least to Locke. English philosophical thought was in fact characterised, precisely from Locke onwards, by the centrality of the gnoseological problem, seen as the study and analysis of the cognitive process in terms of the investigation of the faculties of the mind, in the framework of the empiricist principle according to which all our knowledge derives from experience and in terms of the inspection of the way in which ideas originate in the mind and connect to one another. Thus it has been codified a theory entailing a conception of philosophy as an essentially descriptive study of the actual and factual succession of mental events, investigated according to the canons of Locke's "plain and historical method" that would trace a path followed by English thought for over two hundred years.

Although aware of the psychological implications associated with the notion of meaning[15] Russell developed his reductionist programme on the basis of a conception of language peculiar to the logician and the mathematician in which all problems associated with symbolism fall within and are resolved within the structures of symbolism itself as problems relating to its objective features. It is

---

14   These include, as will be seen below, the discovery of the philosophical relevance of the notion of meaning, its referential conception, the denunciation of the insufficiency of subject-predicate logic, the distinction between logical and grammatical form, the interpretation of identity judgements as tautologies, and the discovery of the hypothetical nature of universal judgements.

15   Cf. Russell, "The Philosophy of logical Atomism" in *Logic and Knowledge* p. 179 ff..

within this framework that we find the theory of purely referential meaning, according to which the meanings of terms are identified with the things or facts they denote. Reference is not conceived as an intentional activity of the speakers, but rather as a function immanent to terms and language.

Bradley and Russell share this view of language, although there are radical differences between the two philosophers, but what needs to be identified for the purposes of our enquiry is the matrix of this rejection of the psychologistic framework that underlies empiricist theory. Bradley does not believe that philosophy is identified with the study of thought and knowledge as it is shown through the examination of images and perceptions. He stands at the opposite side of that physiology of the mind and that reconstruction of the genesis and articulation of representations by which Locke in his *Essay on Human Understanding* intended to investigate the constitution of knowledge from an examination of the functions of the various faculties of the human being.[16]

It is precisely from the rejection of this psychologistic approach underlying Bradley's analysis of the concept of idea that his corrosive critique of empiricist theory of knowledge begins. "In England," he states, "we have lived too long in a psychological attitude"[17]. Empiricists have equated ideas with mental images, thus giving rise to a type of investigation that belongs to psychology rather than to philosophy.

The *idea* studied by philosophy and logic is a different entity from that of psychology. Logic and philosophy deal with judgements and the ideas that form judgements are not psychic entities but 'signs of an existence other than themselves'[18]. For logical and philosophical purposes, we do not consider psychic entities but their meaning; it is not the particular and unrepeatable existence of each representation that we use in judgement, but what it represents. It is the symbolic capacity that interests the philosopher, not the psychic entity that substantiates the symbol; and the symbol is something that stands

---

16 Cf. John. Locke, *Essay on Human Understanding* (London: John Bumpus,1824),vI ed. p.vii
17 F. H. Bradley, *The Principles of Logic* I, p. 2.
18 *ibid.*

for something else: it is a sign that means. If we limit ourselves to considering the representational content, that is, the image present to the mind, we irretrievably miss, according to Bradley, the true essence of the idea, its symbolic character, its aptitude to refer to, to mean.

> A symbol is a fact which stands for something else, and by this we may say, it both loses and gains, is degraded and exalted. In its use as a symbol it forgoes individuality and self existence. It is not the main point that *this* rose or *this* forget-me-not and none other has been chosen. We give it or we take it for the sake of its meaning and that may prove true or false long after the flower has perished.[19]

In all that is we distinguish – this is an especially important distinction in Bradley's logic – the two aspects of *existence* and content. That is, we consider, of everything, that *it is (that)* and what *it is* (what). But signs, symbols have a third aspect: meaning.

A sign, according to Bradley is

> any fact that has meaning and the meaning consists of a part of the content (original or acquired) cut out, fixed by the mind and considered independently of the existence of the sign.[20]

The psychological image or idea, for logic, is nothing but a sensible reality; it is on the same level as *sensations;* both are facts and neither is a meaning; they have existence; they are not thought but given. But an idea, if we use the idea as meaning, is neither given nor presented, it is taken; and it cannot exist as such.[21] These quotations should make it clear how Bradley first drew attention to meaning in the Anglo-Saxon world. The importance of the polarisation of research on the problem of meaning was enormous. All subsequent British philosophy is practically founded on that 'linguistic turn', which has here an unquestionable forerunner.

As far as our specific topic is concerned, it should be noted that Russell's philosophy, appears to be closely linked to this issue, of

---

19   F. H. Bradley, *The Principles of Logic,* vol. I, p.3.
20   *ibid,* p. 4.
21   Bradley, *Principles* p. 7.

which he is certainly one of the main proponents along with Frege. It remains to be seen whether, and to what extent, it is possible to state an at least partial Bradleyan derivation of this whole issue. As is well known, Russell has always acknowledged Frege and Peano as his masters in this regard, but he never did the same with Bradley.

The repudiation of the psychologistic attitude and the attention paid to the problem of meaning appear to be the antecedents of the logical-analytical basis that supports all Russell's thought. The attempt to reconstruct Hume's atomism on a logical register has as its prerequisite precisely the critical analysis of the concept of idea carried out by Bradley with the corollary of the specifically philosophical character of the investigation of meaning. The fundamental stages of Russell's thought corresponding to the publication of *Principles of Mathematics* and the *Philosophy of Logical Atomism* are in fact punctuated precisely by changes in his theory of meaning, which is the core of both his theory of knowledge and his ontology.

As far back as 1903 he had stated that

> Although a grammatical distinction cannot be uncritically to correspond to a genuine philosophical difference yet the one is *prima facie* evidence of the other [...]and that it must be admitted I think that every word occurring in a sentence must have *some* meaning.[22]

In the same context he quoted Bradley's famous distinction between existence and content, between the *What* and the *That.* And it would be precisely the then strictly referential theory of meaning that would provide the rationale for the platonising ontology he would later abandon in the wake of a new theory of meaning.

> Whatever may be an object of thought, or may occur in any true or false proposition, or can be counted as *one* I shall call a *term.* This then is the widest word in the philosophical vocabulary. I shall use as synonymous with it the words unit, individual and entity. The first two emphasize the fact that every term is *one,* while the third is derived from the fact that every term has being, i.e. *is* in some sense.[23]

---

22   B. Russell, *The Principles of Mathematics* p. 42.
23   B.Russell, ibid., p. 43.

This redundant universe was doomed, as we have shown, to undergo a severe downsizing, whose tools are to be found in the epistemological level and in the rigorous application of Ockham's razor, but also in the logical level of a new theory of meaning, advanced in 1905 and known as the *theory of descriptions.*

The Theory of descriptions first appeared in an article entitled *On Denoting*[24] where rejecting both Meinong's views on negative existents[25] and the Fregean distinction of sense and meaning, Russell corrected his primitive belief that in a signifying utterance each component has a meaning even *when* taken in isolation, i.e., according to the referential conception of meaning, amounts to affirm that it has an ontological counterpart. He distinguished two types of symbols: simple symbols and complex symbols, names and descriptions.

The core of the distinction, as it is well known is that while proper names *(logical proper names)* directly denote an object, which constitute their meaning on pain of ceasing to be names, descriptions, which are complex symbols being composed of other symbols, are "apparent names". They may have no meaning when taken in isolation while contributing to the meaning of the proposition in which they occur. The analysis of descriptive sentences made use above all of the fundamental distinction between grammatical subjects and logical subjects, a distinction which, as we shall see, has a precise antecedent in Bradley.

It is of no interest to reconstruct here Russell's theories in detail but to indicate how at the basis of some of them there is on the one hand the assimilation of Bradley's anti-psychologistic polemic and on the other hand, but the two are closely interconnected, the appropriation and development of the issue of meaning that underlies the reconstruction of empiricism in a logical key. Now Russell has always credited Frege with first drawing philosophers'

---

24 Mind, XIV, 1905, pp. 473-493, reprinted in *Logic and knowledge* (London, 1956.

25 An interesting resumption of the debate on non exixtent entities can be found in ; Carolyn. Swanson*, ; Reburial of Nonexistents reconsidering the Meinong-Russell debate*(, Amsterdam ; New York, NY : Rodopi, 2011

attention to the problem of meaning[26] while completely neglecting Bradley's contribution. There is, however, one circumstance that casts a considerable shadow of inaccuracy on this version.

Russell's first contact with Frege's works came after he obtained his professorship and in any case after 1893. On the other hand, it is now established that he read and carefully meticulously annotated Bradley's *Principles of Logic* as early as 1893,[27] Since. as we have seen, Bradley's entire polemic against empiricist gnoseology centres on the relevance of meaning for philosophical analysis, it cannot have gone unnoticed by the young Russell. It is therefore reasonable to think that Russell drew from Bradley's *Logic* fundamental stimuli and inspirations that later flowed into a more mature and articulate lesson than Bradley's, into his analysis of meaning and, more generally, into his approach to philosophical method as an analytical logical method. This view appears, moreover, supported by the private correspondence between the two philosophers.[28] Such considerations do not, however, exhaust the proposed topic; indeed, it is possible identify other themes where recognise a direct and positive influence of Bradley's logic on Russellian theories.

One of the indirect ways Bradley arrives at the statement of the Absolute is through the attempt to show the total incommensurability of discursive thought with respect to reality; this attempt includes the analysis aimed at denouncing the fallacy and contradictory nature of syllogistic inferences and of traditional logic as a whole. Again, we will not go into the sometimes cumbersome details of Bradley's treatment, as it is out of our purpose to analyse it in detail. This enquiry is primarily committed to shed some light on whether and to what extent we can reconstruct an otherwise positive function of his. thought in the general framework of the development of Russellian

---

26   See *My Philosophical Development*, pp.30., 51-53

27   Cf. *My Philosophical Development, cit. and The Autobiography of Bertrand Russell'*see also C. N. Keen, "The Interaction of Russell and Bradley", pp. 8,11. And particularly M.Chalmers and Nicholas Griffin,'s *Russell's Marginalia in his copy of Bradley's Principles of Logic in* Russell vol..17 (1997 N. 1), pp. 1-96

28   See footnote 48

philosophy. We will therefore limit ourselves to indicating those points that illustrate this hypothesis.

One of these points is Bradley's, criticism of the syllogism. He states that the syllogism is insufficient and inadequate because it cannot cover all forms of reasoning.

> The syllogism, he writes, is a chimaera for it professes to be the model of reasoning and there are reasonings which can not by any fair means be conformed to its pattern.[29]

Among the reasonings that do not fall within the syllogistic structure enumerated by Bradley, of particular importance are those based on relations: relations of identity, of quality, of time, of space. Reasoning such as the following: A is to the right of B, B is to the right of C; therefore A is to the right of C cannot in any way be reduced, according to Bradley, to syllogistic schemes. In fact, no judgement appears in it that can act as a major premise and the spatial relation cannot, moreover, be reduced to predication.[30] It is difficult to exaggerate the weight that these observations exert on] Russell's thought.

It was on the discovery of the inadequacy of classical logic to cover relational inferences that Russell grounded his logic of relations which, in turn, underlies the affirmation of pluralism that underpins his ontology and the refutation of all monist metaphysics that paradoxically overwhelmed Bradley's, first among others. Certainly those who approach Bradley's thought through Russell's filter would never suspect the presence of such a rich and keen logical analysis. Indeed, traditional logic finds in Bradley an equally severe critic of symbolic logicians; even if the specificity of his analysis is to be sought beyond logic, in its metaphysics; unlike the logicians and philosophers who were to practise after him the 'therapeutic' analysis of language, he does not mean to provide alternative and more correct analyses. Its purpose is entirely critical and and *destruens* and aims to show the total inability of language to grasp reality.

---

29   F.H. Bradley, *The Principles of Logic* vol. I, p. 248.
30   *The principles*, 246 ff.

Thus Bradley conveyed to Russell the fundamental teaching that the impossibility of making relational reasoning fit into the syllogistic scheme is a consequence of the fact that it is in fact only valid for connecting in deductive chains judgements of the subject-predicate form, while its rules are inapplicable to deductions of judgements that do not fit into this class.

However, classical logic has upheld the thesis according to which propositions are constituted by the attribution of a predicate to a subject and, consequently, the rejection of the exhaustiveness of deductive inference is inseparably connected with the rejection of the view according to which all propositions are formed by a subject and a predicate or can be reduced to subject-predicate propositions. But even this, which is among the most peculiar principles of Russellian logic, is amply supported by Bradley, when he states, with regard to syllogistic inference.

> It is evident that this principle of reasoning is valid but it will not cover the whole of the ground; for, confined to the category of subject and attribute it fails wherever you pass beyond. The subject is in some way qualified by whatever can be asserted about any of his attributes, but it is idle to expect a result from this where we are not concerned with subject and attribute; 'A is prior to B' and 'B to C' and therefore 'A is prior to C'... But what here am I to call 'the condition of the rule' or the '*nota*' or 'attribute'?[31]

As early as chapter I of his *Logic*, Bradley asserted the impossibility of fitting all propositions into the subject-predicate scheme:

> The ideal complex, asserted or denied no doubt in most cases, will fall int the arrangement of a subject with adjectival qualities, but in certain instances, and those not a few, the content takes the form of two or more subjects with adjectival relations between them.[32]

---

31 F. H. Bradley, *The Principles of Logic,*p. 250. The reference is to the Kantian maxim that what is subject to the condition of the rule is subject to the rule.

32 *ibid,* p. 22.

And in addition to relational propositions, Bradley considered other types of propositions irreducible to the subject-predicate structure, primarily the existential and negative judgements that he considered "difficult to persuade" within the afore mentioned scheme.

It is of little relevance in this context to note that the intimately critical rather than positive character of his thought and the subordinate office of logic to the statement of the metaphysical doctrine of the Absolute later led Bradley to reintroduce the thesis that all propositions are of the subject-predicate form. What is significant, however, is the unequivocal fact that he clearly stated as early as 1883 the irreducibility of all propositions to the predicative structure and that Russell read and reflected on this work at length.

In Chapter XXVI of the *Principles of Mathematics* of 1903, he sets out in a mature version his conception of external relations that had first appeared three years earlier in his book on Leibniz's philosophy:

> It is a common opinion – often held unconsciously and employed in argument, even by those who do not explicitly advocate it –, that all propositions ultimately, consist of a subject and a predicate. When this opinion is confronted by a relational proposition, it has two ways of dealing with it, of which the one may be called monadistic, the other monistic. Given, say, the proposition *aRb,* where *R* is some relation, the monadistic view will analyse this into two propositions, which we may call *a*r 1 and *b*r2, which give to *a* and to *b* respectively adjectives supposed to be together equivalent to *R. The* monistic view, on the contrary, regards the relation as a property of the whole composed of *a* and *b,* and as thus equivalent to a proposition which we may denote by *(ab)*r. Of these views, the first is represented by Leibniz, and (on the whole) by Lotze, the second by Spinoza and Mr Bradley.[33]

In fact, as we have seen, the distinction of the different forms of propositions had not escaped Bradley at all. He had rejected it in *Appearance and Reality,* after having considered it in his *Logic,* like all discursive thought and language, as absolutely unsuitable for grasping the true unitary structure of reality and if anything confined

---

33   Russell, *The Principles of Mathematics,* p. 221.

to describing appearance alone. But both here and in the many other places in which he deals with the structural connection between metaphysical substance-attribute and subject-predicate logic[34] Russell almost always quotes *Appearance and Reality* to refute the monist doctrine, conversely unjustly leaving in the shade the *logic* that appears the most significant and which he had, as we have seen, carefully studied and assimilated.

The subject-predicate structure is, however, only one aspect of the more general issue of the logical form of propositions.The difference between an assertion such as "A is to the left of B" and "Tom is tall" is in fact a difference in logical form concealed by the apparent identity of grammatical form. Now, the analytical component of Russellian philosophy consists of a set of techniques aimed at explicating the true logical form of propositions concealed by the imprecise and misleading grammatical form in natural languages; the analysis acquires therefore its philosophical character from the metaphysical hypothesis of isomorphism.

This is a latest version of empiricist reductionism; while the classical empiricism operated on ideas, seen as representations, and was thus marked by psychologistic forms, this one operates on propositions and has an eminently logical structure. Russell's and Wittgenstein's logical atomism and, within it, the project of an ideal language and, specifically, the theory of descriptions fall within this framework of the reduction of utterances to their logical form.

The notion of logical form appears, therefore, as one of the cornerstones of Russell's philosophy; both the analysis of propositions and its ontology are centred on it. When he stated in the essay 'Logical Atomism' – page 330 – that

> the influence of language on philosophy has, I believe, been profound and almost unrecognized, If we are not to be misled by this influence it is necessary to become conscious and to ask ourselves deliberately how far it is legitimate.

---

34   Cf. *The Problems of Philosophy* p. 57 and *Our knowledge of The External World.*, p. 47.

he actually meant to maintain that our ontology is more or less directly determined by the structure of propositions and that therefore the method for deriving a correct ontological vision passes through the explication of the true logical form of propositions.

Even the notion of logical form and its distinction from grammatical form can be traced in Bradley's logic, who seems to have been quite aware of the issue connected to it and, in any case, not really inclined to 'succumb to subject-predicate logic' as one would be led to believe on the basis of Russellian writings alone. In introducing this theme and almost warning the reader against the pitfall that can lurk behind the apparent structure of language. Russell warns that

> almost every proposition can be expressed in a form in which it is composed of a subject and a predicate joined by a copula, – and that – it is natural to infer from this that every fact must have a corresponding form and must thus consist in the possession of a quality by a substance. This naturally leads to monism [...].[35]

Actually, Bradley had not been led to monism inadvertently by his failure to evaluate the logical structure of language; it seems, on the contrary, that he was clearly acquainted with this issue if we are to judge from certain passages of his *Logic,* which, as always, does not constitute the direct term of reference of Russellian polemic. Indeed, he states that

> I admit you may torture the matter from the second form into the first. But if torture is admitted, the enquiry will become a mere struggle between torturers.[36]

Russell based much of his methodology on the notion of logical form understood as the structure of the proposition independent of content. This notion he claims to have taken from the work of Peano and Frege.[37] His first contact with Peano dates back, as is well known, to 1900, the date of the International Congress of Philosophy in Paris, while his contact with Frege's work is even later. We still

---

35   *Logical Atomism,* in Logic and Knowledge p. 331
36   Cf. F. H. Bradley, *The Principles of Logic,* p. 22.
37   Cf. *Our Knowledge of the External World,* pp. 50-1.

recall that he had, however, carefully studied Bradley's Logic since 1893 and that it had "profoundly influenced" him. In the first chapter of this work Bradley clearly distinguishes these two aspects. In his analysis of the proposition he also clearly separates the *grammatical* subject from the ultimate subject:

> by subject I mean here not the ultimate subject to which the entire ideal content refers but the subject that is part of that content, in other words the grammatical subject.[38]

And this subject is not actually what the predicate refers to. Although such a theory is to be framed within Bradley's conception of the inability of singular judgements to grasp facts, and refers to the conception according to which all judgements are in fact hypothetical and their true structure is that of categorical assertions about reality taken as a whole. The sole true subject of all judgements -this is his drastic conclusion, which ultimately eliminates the very possibility of judgement – does not affect Bradley's intuition of the need to distinguish logical form from grammatical form. Indeed, when Bradley claims that a statement such as "the grass is green" mean in truth "reality is such that the grass is green" or when he analyses negative propositions such as "the round square does not exist" by reducing and transcribing them into "the nature of space excludes the connection of square and round"[39] he is not far away from the problematic of Russell's analysis of "the golden mountain does not exist" or "the king of France is bald". His assertion that "it is not the pure and casual conjunction of any proposition that represents reality, but in every proposition the analysis of meaning will find a reality of which something is affirmed or denied", appears extraordinarily close to the Russellian thesis that in a proposition such as "The golden mountain does not exist", the analysis points out that the golden mountain is not the actual subject of the proposition and therefore the predicate does not refer to it.[40] Again, Russell stated that he learned from Frege the distinction between meaning and

---

38   F. H. Bradley, The Principles 1 of Logic. p. 22.
39   *Ibid,* p. 42
40   Cf. B.Russell, *On Denoting,* p. 45 ff.

denotation but there is no doubt that the distinction between logical subject and grammatical subject and thus the distinction of logical form from grammatical form is traceable in Bradley's logic which cannot but have influenced the subsequent outcomes of his analysis.

Another Bradleyan thesis that will only acquire a relevant character and development within Russellian philosophy is the analysis of the general propositions of the form 'all A's are B'.

Bradley's attempt to reject empiricist pluralism records among its most brilliant expedients the development of a numerous series of arguments aimed at showing the impossibility of the linguistic grasping of the single, particular fact which is the elementary unity of empiricist gnoseology.

To this end, he argues his thesis of language's inability to designate unambiguously. The second chapter of his *Logic* is in fact occupied by a review of the forms of judgement, in a polemical attempt to trace (or perhaps it would be more accurate to say exhibit non-traceability) the form that the particular judgement of fact assumes. It will not be necessary to retrace the various stages of this meticulous but always acute analysis here; it will suffice to briefly recall its outcomes. All forms of judgement are examined and rejected one after another. The negative judgement, Bradley argues, cannot be identified with the empiricists' judgement of fact, because a judgement such as 'A is not B', far from asserting the particular fact, rather says that it is not a fact, and thus lacks an ontological reference[41]. The hypothetical judgement of the form "If A is B, C will be D" cannot, either, be identified with the singular judgement. This judgement, in fact, does not assert a singular, particular fact; the fulfilment of the component propositions (A is B, and C is D), i.e. their actual assertion of a fact, does not condition its overall truth, and it cannot, *a fortiori, be* asserted to assert something.

The judgement of fact moreover is not identified with the disjunctive one, of the form 'A is B or C'. It is rejected with reasons and arguments similar to those with which he rejected the negative judgement, namely the impossibility of tracing an

---

41   Cf. F.H. Bradley, *The Principles of Logic,* vol. I, p. 46 ff. Interestingly, Russell later admitted to some extent, the existence of negative facts

ontological counterpart, due to the non-existence of disjunctive facts corresponding to it. Bradley finally examines the universal judgements of the form 'all A's are B', and it is precisely the analysis of these that is of particular importance within the debate on relations between Bradley and Russell. He analysed these judgements in terms of generalisations of hypothetical judgements. The core and the conclusion of Bradley's view is that the analysis finally result is that all judgements are hypothetical, and they are hypothetical in the sense that they have only an indirect reference to reality, to the facts that empiricists believe, in their view, erroneously, that they can unambiguously designate through them. Language, on the other hand, does not, in his view, allow unambiguous and direct reference to partial sectors of experience. Nonetheless, they have also a categorial character insofar as each judgement, although not representing its apparent subject, constitutes a categorial statement on Reality taken as a *whole*. The correct analysis of judgements such as *'this horse is white'* would be, according to Bradley, *'Reality is such that this horse is white'*.

'All A's are B' does not in fact assert the existence of any of the objects indicated by the subject; it does not say, in other words, that there are A's. The universal plural subject does not have a circumscribable *denotatum*; it refers to all possible A's, past, present and future,[42] to the whole open class. In a judgement such as 'Animals are mortal' we do not mean that whatever is an animal will die; but this is equivalent to *If* something is an animal, *then it* will die. The assertion is in fact about a hypothetical conjunction of predicates and not about a fact.[43] Unlike the particular judgement, the universal judgement represents a relation between universal predicates. 'All animals are mortal' says nothing about animals, but merely exhibits the compatibility, indeed the implication, of animal and mortal. It would remain true even if there were no animals. The psychological attitude of considering the synthesis of adjectives expressed by universal judgements as existing in fact, in no way determines their actual conjunction in reality. In his intellectual autobiography, Russell

---

42   *ibid.* p. 47 ff.
43   *ibid. cit.*

observes that his main logical progress stems from his awareness of the distinction between utterances of the form 'Socrates is mortal' and utterances of the form 'All Greeks are mortal'.

The following quotation shows beyond doubt how the thesis that Russell attributed to Peano, and to which he traced a fundamental advancement of his own; is in fact the same one that Bradley had long since enunciated:

> "All Greeks are mortal" expresses a relation of two predicates, – viz 'Greek' and 'mortal'. The full statement of "All Greeks are mortal" is: "For all possible values of x, if x is Greek, x is mortal". We have here, instead of a subject-predicate proposition, a connection of two propositional functions, each of which becomes a subject-predicate proposition when a value is assigned to the variable x. The statement "All Greeks are mortal" says nothing about Greeks in particular but is a statement about everything in the universe. The statement "If x is Greek, x is mortal" is just as true when x is not Greek and when x is Greek. Indeed, it is true if there are no Greeks at all. "All Lilliputians are mortal" is true although there are no Lilliputians. The statement 'all Greeks are mortal' unlike the statement 'Socrates is mortal' names no one and expresses only and solely a connection of predicates.[44]

Russell's assertion that universal propositions cannot be proved by enumeration is equivalent to Bradley's view that the word "all" is equivalent to anything and therefore it implies "if". The thesis of the character not of propositions but of enunciative functions of expressions containing the word "all" is clearly stated by Bradley and the only relevant difference is the absence, in his analysis, of the explicit use of variables.

We have here a further case of a singular refusal of inheritance.

A confirm of the singularity of Russell's attitude in this matter is the last letter sent to him by Bradley, in which the old philosopher, who had practically survived his philosophy, lamented the failure

---

44   B. Russell, *My Philosophical Development* p. 52. The textual match of Russell's intellectual autobiography with Bradley's *Logic* is striking. The latter bears a very advanced analysis of universal utterances in terms of hypothetical utterances, an analysis that is known to substantiate large sections of Russell's logic.

by Russell to recognise his intellectual debt. But the controversy between the two philosophers draws its fullest significance in the dispute over the nature of relations.

> I have always believed, Bradley wrote to Russell on 27 September 1914, "that in 1883, in my logic, I indicated a number of inferences which could not be ascribed to the categories of subject and attribute, and I also indicated that there was, nevertheless, a form in every possible inference. I do not intend to claim originality for anything since I have read many writers of various schools and my memory is so fragile that it is possible for me to remember something without being aware of its source or even having a source. I believe, however, that these points were undoubtedly expressed in my book of 1883.
>
> You, on the other hand, seem to assert that they only became known with Peano and Frege, of course with much more explicitness.
>
> Now, even if this had happened in 1883. I cannot understand how I could have known about it either directly or indirectly; certainly no one could have been less of a mathematician than I.
>
> So why should I not have been given any credit even if Peano and Frege had dealt with *it* before me? I may, however, have misunderstood it and in any case it is only a small matter of history without any importance.[45]

Here two worldviews and two ways of doing philosophy find their fullest expressions. One wonders how different these two conceptions are and whether they are actually as irreconcilable as they seem at first sight. There are those who describe, and perhaps not wrongly, this clash more as the diffraction of the same image than as authentic opposition"[46].

---

45 Cf. C.N. Keen, "The interaction", cit., pp. 10-1.
46 J. Passmore, *Russell and Bradley,* pp. 21-30, particularly p. 29.

CHAPTER THREE
RELATIONS AND PLURALISM

Russell's theory of relations is not only the core of the revolutionary logical-mathematical treatment of the subject offered in the *Principia*, but also the point of arrival of a refutation of the idealist and monist worldview. It is the ground on which these two images of the world opposed to one another.

Tracing back this dispute and the arguments brought against the monist conception of relations, we are especially interested in showing the shaping of the pluralist instance that constitutes the first element of future Russell's theory of logical atomism.

Bradley's view that the only reality is the Absolute, is based, according Russell, on an erroneous conception of relations that he calls the 'theory of internal relations'. Every relational fact in Bradleyan version of monism is intrinsic to the nature of the terms that enter into the relation and of the whole considered, i.e. something like an "adjective" of them. In the relation "*A* is to the left of *B*", for example, the relation "to the left of" and "to the right of" would be part either of the nature of the complex made up by *A* and B or of the terms considered individually, whereas the relation, as such, would not have any reality of its own.

The consequences of this theory, especially the epistemological ones, seemed to Russell totally unacceptable and to be necessarily refuted. We'll try to reconstruct in some more detail the terms of the dispute to highlight its true nature, that is, the clash, between two incompatible ontologies.

The core of Bradley's worldview is the theory according to which the multiplicity of substances, of entities, is only the deceptive subjective reflex of a single substance, the *Absolute*, which is only one and indivisible.

This ontology which amounts to a radical monism follows a critical reasoning substantiated by a series of rejections: rejection of the testimony of the senses; of the validity of analysis as a method of investigation; rejection of the power of language to univocally designate parts of the reality and, therefore, to express partial contents of experience; rejection of considering what appears complex as consisting of simple elements. Bradley represents a diametrically opposed theoretical, ontological and methodological view with respect to Russell's. According to Russell the understanding of the distinct aspects of reality is linked to the possibility of its breakdown into its simple elements in view of the possible subsequent reconstruction of the compounds; and this applies to both on the side of language and of sensory perception. Bradley stands at the opposite side of this conception.

The attempt at an analysis, purporting the disarticulation of the complexes into their simple constituent elements, results – in his opinion – in an inexorable failure. The condition of significance of the parts resides for him, invariably in the whole that they make up and any attempt to break them down only takes us away from an adequate understanding.

To understand the parts, it is necessary to understand the whole in which they are integrated; the division into parts itself does not give us reality, but only ephemeral, deceptive appearances that reflect 'our ignorance elevated to reality'.[1] Unfortunately, while the objective content of his theses is clear, the arguments put forward in support of them, although of great suggestive force, are for the most part extremely obscure and vitiated by frequent transpositions of the results of psychological approach onto the ontological plane.

---

1   The passionate rejection of the testimony of the senses, as fallacious and contradictory, constitutive, that is, of appearance, runs throughout *Appearance and Reality*. Even where the topic of relations is not specifically under discussion, it is, always, in the background insofar as the entire work is pervaded by the deceptive reciprocal reduction of qualities to relations and vice versa. It is therefore impossible or extremely difficult to quote all the specific places of the relational theme; it is, however, most present in the chapter dedicated to *Noun and Adjective* and in the one entitled *Relations and Qualities*. See also pp. 362ff. and 419 ff.

This is particularly surprising if one considers that Bradley was one of the main proponents of the need to clearly distinguish empirical psychology from philosophy and based on this distinction a sharp and fruitful critique of the empiricist theory of knowledge[2]. His philosophy is a polemical and critical construction that reaches monist ontological conclusions only indirectly, through an attempt at *reductio ad absurdum* of the assumptions on which pluralism rests. This makes his thought difficult to summarise and insinuates the feeling, supported on a theoretical level by the assumption of the incommensurability of thought to reality[3], that he regarded with a certain contempt the need to use an ultimately incongruous instrument to affirm his truth.

All his arguments share, to some extent, the fate of Wittgenstein's ladder. We will not, however, deal separately with his many suggestive interpretations and examples of how the *Whole* can be mutilated through language or his conception of the unreality of space, time, etc. We will focus on the main argument put forward against a pluralist worldview: the theory of internal relations also and above all because this is the ground on which Russell bases his rejection and refutation of monism. It is possible to succinctly express the thesis of internal relations by stating the analytical and *a priori* character of all propositions that attribute a relation to a term.

The multiplicity of objects and events witnessed by the experience seem to postulate, on the one hand, the autonomous existence of many of these objects and events and, correlatively, the occurrence between them of various and many spatial, temporal relations. Thus we will say that "A precedes B"; that "C is to the left of D"; and that "E loves F". These relations appear to be of two fundamental types; some are intimately rooted in the nature of the term such that if it did not have that relation 'it would be different from what it is in

---

2   Cf. On this issue ch. II. The whole development of Russell's thought has shown, moreover, the fruitfulness and efficacy of this critique, whose history is at the origin of some fundamental developments in subsequent research on science. One may think, in this regard, to the controversial distinction between the context of discovery and the context of justification.

3   See on this point footnote 6 in Chapter I.

qualitative as well as numerical terms. The relation exemplified by the word 'married' for instance is internal with respect to the term 'husband' but external with respect to 'man'.

The proposition saying that a certain husband is married is thus an analytical proposition, true *a priori,* tautological. Its truth results, in fact, from the mere definition of the subject. No one could be a husband without being married; the lack of such a relation would thus constitute a qualitative as well as a numerical difference and would be constitutive of a contradiction. If, on the other hand, the husband in question was also a member of a yachting club, this further relationship would be external; it could not be deduced from an analysis of the meaning of the term or the nature of the subject, configuring rather an entirely contingent and extrinsic fact. The husband in question could also not be a member of the yachting club without being another individual, i.e. without an intrinsic difference in his nature, but he could not have been a bachelor.

Another way of posing the distinction of relations into internal and external can be as follows: when we ask whether a certain relation is internal or external with respect to a term, we ask ourselves about the link that connects an expression designating a class or a universal (husband) to the set of characteristics that define it, to its connotation, i.e. to its necessary predicates. If the relation under scrutiny falls within the set of such necessary characteristics, it will be internal, in all other cases it will be purely external and contingent. Thus, while being married is a feature that falls within the set that defines necessarily the class of, husbands, i.e. the universal *husband* and thus constitutes an internal relation, the membership to the yacht club certainly does not fall within it and thus constitutes a merely external relation. The internal or external nature of the relation is determined, again, by the nature of the link that connects a universal to an individual, through one or more definitions.

British idealists[4] and in particular Bradley rejected this interpretation of relations and it is easy to see why.

---

4   British idealism landscape is very complex and articulated and even on the interpretation of relations there is no lack of divergences. Significant, in this regard, is the position of Thomas H. Green who, – in his Introduction

The distinction of relations into internal and external, agrees with common sense and is fundamental and necessary to any pluralist ontology. If all relations were internal, i.e. were founded on terms and, in turn, on the nature of the terms, no entity could exist independently of the others; the nature of each thing would necessarily be constituted by its relations to the others, and since from each individual object or event one would pass through its relations to the others with which it is connected (and of which it is therefore a part) and from these, in turn, to the others with which they are related, it would be impossible to distinguish each thing or event from the others.

This accounts for the fact that one would necessarily arrive at the existence of only one thing; precisely at ontological monism. The close functional link between the doctrine of internal relations and monism is thus understood, and it also explains why the Bradleyan denial of external relations constitutes a powerful argument against pluralism. But let us look in some more detail at the content of monist arguments and their structure.

The core of the thesis asserted is that relations do not have an autonomous status; they are not components of the world to be counted alongside terms. On this fundamental assumption, to which we will return, is grafted the conception that sees relations as expressing *qualities* of the related terms or of the whole that they contribute to compose. The arguments put forward by Bradley in support of his thesis are of two kinds: some of a general philosophical nature, others in the 'form of *reductio ad absurdum* of the opposing theses.

The first argument against external relations is based on a sharp distinction of great weight throughout Bradley's thought, that between *characters* and *existing things*. If we take, for example, a number of

---

of Hume's *Treatise* of 1874 – although resolves the reality in an absolute consciousness, interprets it as a net of relations risking unintelligibility and ineffability. To be real – says Green – or to be a fact is to be a 'phenomenon' something that is given to us in experience; but the minimum that we experience is always a set of relations. Here the apparent alignment with empiricist theses ceases because relations are for Green a work of the mind, that is, they exist only for a sentient consciousness.

objects arranged in space, say, chess pieces on a chessboard and two players, we notice that each of the pieces and the two men are in a certain spatial relation with one another.

If one of the men subsequently moves or one of the pieces is moved, its spatial relations to the other objects will *eo ipso* be altered. Now although everyone agrees that the spatial change of a chess piece has entailed a modification for it, i.e. has changed it in the sense that it has altered its spatial relations with all other objects, not everyone would argue, against common sense, that with the change of place and thus with the change of its spatial relations the chess piece has undergone an intrinsic change in its nature. Among them is Bradley.

Referring to the previous arguments, one could say that the spatial position, although it could be considered as a property of the piece, is not among those defining the universal 'chess piece', i.e. it is not among the characteristics necessarily connected with its description. Bradley's attitude in the face of these considerations is quite singular: he accepts their validity but then immediately rejects their relevance. In other words, the reasoning, although formally correct, rests on erroneous or irrelevant premises. It is possible – he argues – to distinguish relations into internal and external ones, only because pluralists conceive of objects not as they really are, i.e. unique, unrepeatable and therefore intrinsically determined by their relations, but as *genera* of things, clusters of properties of which some are taken into account rather than others in a completely arbitrary and illegitimate process of abstraction.

> For a thing may remain unaltered, he argues, if you identify it with a certain character, while taken otherwise is suffering change. If, that is you take, a billiard ball and a man, in abstraction from place, they will of course – so far as this is maintained – be indifferent to changes of place […] but take them as existing things and take them without mutilation, and you must regard them as determined by their places and qualified by the whole material system into which they enter […] The billiard-ball, to repeat if taken apart from the place and its position in the whole is not an existence but a character, and that character can

remain unchanged, though the existing thing is altered by its changed existence.[5]

This interpretation sheds light on a fundamental feature of Bradley's thesis, namely the systematic assimilation of relations to properties already mentioned, as well as the reduction of relationality to predication; this assimilation supports, on the one hand, the assertion that all relations are internal and – linked to this though distinct from it – the thesis that wants terms to be intrinsically modified by relations[6] so that the possession of a property is identified with the existence of a relation between two or more terms.

> The relation, Bradley asserts, is not identical with the thing. It is only a kind -of *attribute that is* inherent to it or belongs to it.[7]

and the relation always entails a substantial foundation in the terms.

The second of the general arguments in favour of internal relations is what Russell considered a singular interpretation of the principle of sufficient reason. Bradley argued that each thing, and therefore also relations, must have some reason for subsisting rather than not subsisting; applied to relations this reasoning implies that if the relation does not qualify its terms it would be useless and arbitrary and completely meaningless.

> If terms do not by their own internal nature enter into the relation, the relation as far as they are concerned seems entirely arbitrary (*ibid.*, p. 392).

Since such arbitrariness seemed inconceivable to him, he deduced a grounding of relations in the nature of terms. Alongside these general objections, Bradley will make some more specific

---

5   F.H.Bradley, *Appearance and Reality, appendix* p. 578.

6   On this aspect of Bradley's theory see George E. Moore, "External and Internal Relations" in *Proceedings* of the *Aristotelian Society,* vol. XX, 1919-20 pp. 40-62, reprinted in *Philosophical Studies (*London, Kegan Paul,1922, pp. 276-309.

7   F. H. Bradley, *Appearance and Reality* p. 20

criticisms in an attempt to reduce the opposing thesis to absurdity or contradiction.

He first tries to prove that terms are inconceivable without relations and relations without terms, and then he argues for the opposite view according to which terms are incompatible with relations and relations are incompatible with terms. The entire argument actually turns out to be directed not so much at the affirmation of internal relations as at the exhibition of the unintelligibility and contradictory nature of the relational nexus as such, and thus at the assertion of the impossibility of both internal and external relations on which all pluralist ontology rests.

Relations subsist between terms, but for this to be possible, Bradley believes, they must be inherent to the terms, and this inherence can only be ensured by a new relation that connects the first relation to the terms; thus when two terms are in relation, there cannot only be the terms and the relation but also a further relation between each of the terms and the first relation. Naturally, the same problem arises for new relations, thus initiating a process to infinity

> But here, again, he says, we are hurried off into the eddy of a hopeless process, since we are forced to go on finding new relations without end. The links are united by a link and this bond of union is a link which also has two ends; and these require each a fresh link to connect them to the old. The problem is to find how the relations can stand to its qualities; and this problem is insoluble. (*ibid.*, p. 33)

To an exam of the arguments with which Russell rejected this conception of relations, it must be premised that in the framework of Bradleyan monism the defence of internal relations constitutes, as we have already mentioned, an outpost of the more radical rejection of relations *tout court*. It is the very distinction between terms and relations that is called into question. It expresses, in his view, the mutilation of reality that we operate by elevating our subjective limits to reality.

> The arrangement of given facts into relations and qualities, says Bradley, may be necessary in practice, but it is theoretically

unintelligible. The reality so characterised is not true reality but is appearance. (*ibid.*, p. 25)

Terms, relations, as well as space, time and things in time and space have no substantiality; they are merely abstractions from the Whole, which they cannot express, so that in an inventory of the world not only the external relations but also the internal ones would find no place. Moreover, this inventory would record in Bradley's ontological accounts only one item, the Absolute.

Internal relations cannot, on closer inspection, be considered relations in the proper sense. The very concept of internal relation appears ambiguous and contradictory; when the relation is conceived as internal, it cannot be identified as other than the term, nor can the term be considered independently of it.

In a world of internal relations, any discourse around the relational nexus in its specificity would necessarily fall down and any reference to its ontological autonomy – on which, in pluralism the distinction of realities rests – would loose meaning.[8]

In fact, Bradley was aware of the untenability of many of his arguments as the Russellian critique would later highlight; however, this should not have unduly upset him. The precariousness of various attempts to assimilate relations to qualities and the consequent defence of internal relations presents two interesting but distinct aspects. We have seen that Bradley did not mean to defend internal relations as such; he supported this thesis, because it was necessary in its general lines to a vision of reality as a whole, in which the attempts to isolate and guarantee autonomy to the parts, as configured in the doctrine of external relations, appeared contradictory to him. The explication of this contradiction passed through the statement of the internality of relations; if then even the internal relations turned out to be untenable, this could not be considered a real defeat from his point of view. In fact, it showed not so much the fallacy of his arguments – at least this is what he believed – but to the unintelligibility of relationality as such, with all the ontological

---

8   Cf. William A. Vallicella, 'Monism and the Vindication of Bradley's Regress', *Dialectica* 2002, Vol. 56 N.! (2002) p. 3-35

consequences it entailed. The consequences, namely monism, were, in the framework of his thought, ultimately positive.

It is in this framework that the general conception that underlies all the arguments aimed at showing the other theory according to which relations are attributes not of the individual elements but of the complexes of which the individual terms are part, a thesis that, as we shall see, ends to be the privileged target of Russell's criticism. Throughout his discussion of the problem he actually keeps the question "whether there are independent relations outside some unity" out of the field. The negative answer to this question is in fact for him an unquestionable presupposition.

The refutation of the theory of internal relations appears for the first time in full in *The Principles of Mathematics,* in 1903, and will be developed by Russell in a numerous series of writings[9] almost always in relation to the connection he identifies between this theory and ontological monism. However, the framework within which his arguments fit had already been elaborated at least three years earlier, in the course of his work on Leibniz[10]. In *The Principles of Mathematics*, in 1903, in fact, the analytical logical method of investigation established the relevance of logical-linguistic structures for the investigation of problems of general philosophy and ontology. Leibniz's entire philosophy was therein traced back to a few axioms of a logical nature, but above all Russell established a direct connection between the Leibnizian analysis of the proposition and its metaphysics.

---

9   For the more properly philosophical aspects of the theory see, also: *The Philosophy of Leibniz,* 1971, pp. 8-14; "The Monistic Theory of Truth" in *Philosophical Essays(* London, Longmans, Green & Co,) 1910*; Our Knowledge of the External World, ch. II;* "Philosophy of Logical Atomism" in *Monist, v. 28*, oct. 1918 "Logical Atomism, in Contemporary British Philosophy, Personal Statements, First series(London, George Allen & Unwin,1924) pp. 356-383;repr.in *Logic and Knowledge* pp.335 *ff. Introduction to Mathematical Philosophy* (London, Allen & Unwin, 1919) ch. V; *My Philosophical Development, ch.* V; *Principia Mathematica* (with A. N. Whitehead), 3 vols.(Cambridge, Cambridge University Press, 1910-13, 1925-27²) the place quoted in vol. I part I, sect. C.

10   B. Russell, *The Philosophy of Leibniz,*

This was, in his view, based on the theory – implicit in Leibniz – according to which all propositions are reducible to the subject-predicate form, that constitutes the linguistic correlate, and is perhaps at the origin, of ontologies that analyse facts in terms of *substance* and *accident*. Even then Russell considered this connection to be of extreme importance and far from being limited to Leibniz's philosophy, but constitutive of all metaphysics of the substance.

> The view that a subject and a predicate are to be found in every proposition is a very ancient and respectable doctrine; moreover, it has, by no means lost its hold in philosophy, since Mr Bradley's logic consists almost wholly of the contention that every proposition ascribes a predicate to Reality as the only ultimate subject. (*ibid.*, p. 12)

Since then, Russell suggested, but did not elaborate on the argument, that this reduction was not possible for propositions using mathematical ideas[11] and for relational propositions and advanced the view that the relation is something distinct from subject and accident.

In *Principles of Mathematics* he will set the terms of his interpretation of the relations and of the controversy with the monists destined to drag on for years, as well as in his essays, in the pages of *Mind* and to conclude, or rather to end only with Bradley's death, starting precisely from a passage of Leibniz that had already attracted his attention. Since it thickens all the themes that Russell

---

11   The analysis of mathematical propositions shows, according to Russell, that such propositions cannot be explained unless pluralism is admitted, since in mathematics we must know units before we know anything about their relations to other units, and this would be impossible if relations were part of the terms. "All assertions of numbers, such as e.g. 'There are three men' essentially assert plurality of subjects, though they may also give a predicate to each of the subjects. Such propositions cannot be regarded as a mere sum of subject-predicate propositions, since the number only results from the singleness of the proposition and would be absent if three propositions asserting each the presence of one man' were juxtaposed *ibid.,*p. 12., cf. also *The Principles of Mathematics,* pp. 39-40, 83-84

will later develop and summarises the different interpretations of the relations to which he refers, we will quote it in full:

> The ratio or proportion between two lines, L and M, can be conceived in three several ways; as the ratio of the greater L to the lesser M; as the ratio of the lesser M to the grater L; and lastly as something abstracted from both, that is, as the ratio between L and M, without considering which is the antecedent or which the consequent; which the subject and which the object […]In the first way of considering them, L, the grater, is the subject; in the second, M, the lesser, is the subject of that accident which philosophers call *relation* or *ratio*. But which of them will be the subject in the third way of considering them? It cannot be said that both of them, L and M together, are the subject of such an accident; for if so we should have an accident in two subjects, with one leg in one and the other in the other: which is contrary to the notion of accident. Therefore we must say that this relation, in this third way of considering it, is indeed *out of* the subjects; but being neither a substance nor an accident, it must be a mere ideal thing, the consideration of which is nevertheless useful.[12]

Russell's discussion of relations deals with several issues that, although intertwined, should be considered separately. Considered together, they relate to two fundamental issues: the assertion of the independent reality of relations and the thesis of the external character of relations. Linked to the first of these two issues are the conception of relations as components of the world, their irreducibility to qualities; linked to the second are the logical arguments on their functioning and the logical properties of relations. As we shall see, Russell will

---

12   *Philosophische Werke,* ed. Gerhardt, vol. VII, p. 401, quoted by Russell in *The Philosophy of Leibniz,* pp.12:13. An interesting discussion of Russell's interpretation of Leibniz's theory of relations can be found in M. Mugnai, "Bertrand Russell e il problema delle relazioni in Leibniz" even if it is not always possible to agree with some of the theses on which the author sets out his discussion; e.g. the one for which one rejects the Russell's criticism of the subjectivist interpretation of relations in Leibniz, backing, a possible legitimacy "for a philosopher who admits the existence of God" (C. 359). Although indeed, it seems peculiar to attribute to a belief the strength to *objectively* ground anything.

respond blow by blow to Bradley by addressing the controversy on both general philosophical and logical-linguistic grounds.

The assimilation of relations to properties is the thesis that although Russell attributes fundamentally to the monadists, i.e. Leibniz. is in fact also supported by the monists, when in their defence of internal relations they advance the argument that for a relation to connect a term, it must be inherent to it. By inherence, it should be pointed out, they mean the relation of qualities to the subject.

The distinction of *characters* and *existing things* advanced by Bradley is also an attempt to assimilate relations to properties; an assimilation that can be briefly illustrated in the following way: given a relational function *aRb* it will be reduced to two propositions *ar*[1] *and br*[2] which attribute to *a* and *b* attributes that together are equivalent to the relation *R*. If we consider a quantitative relation such as that expressed by the proposition "A is greater than B" and attempt to reduce the relation to attributes of terms by formulating two propositions, one attributing an attribute to *a* and the other to *b,* we cannot help but observe that the two attributes will be in a reciprocal relation, and if we again attempt to reduce this further relation to further attributes, we shall again have to explain the difference of the attributes. If we attempt to do this with new attributes rather than with a term-independent – i.e. external – relation, we will be giving rise to an inadmissible regress to infinity, no degree of which will come closer to the meaning of the original proposition. Every attribute of the 'referent' of the relation necessarily implies a reference to the corresponding attribute of the *relatum* and vice versa, and this irreducible reference is precisely that relation which monists and monadists intend to deny. In the absence of the external reference, the attribute in no way qualifies the terms considered in isolation. If, for example, one volume is greater than another, one can attempt to explain this proposition by saying that one has the dimensions *x* and the other the dimension *y*. However, this attempt is not conclusive because the respective dimensions will be different, and this difference is precisely a relation between the dimensions. If we attempt to reduce this new relationship to further attributes, such as the number of pages, one will have a greater number of pages than the other and so on ad infinitum, the relation proves irreducible to the property. Nor is any attempt to reduce the asymmetrical relation (such as that of "greater than") to the symmetrical relation of the *diversity of* attributes any better. In this case the proposition that A and *B* have different attributes does not allow us to distinguish which of the two is the greater and which the lesser, i.e. it does not allow us to reconstruct the meaning of the original proposition, which is inextricably linked to the asymmetry of the relation.

Each attribute must have a reference to the other term of the relation; and this is equivalent to the external relation, i.e. independent of the nature of the terms themselves.

The second monist argument rejected by Russell is the claim that the connection of relations with terms requires and implies a further relation and so on, in an infinite regress. Russell rejects this objection on two main grounds: he claims, first, that the whole argument originates and is inspired by a distorted and unacceptable notion of relations, which is fundamentally substantialist in nature. To require that the connection of a term with a relation be ensured by another relation is to precisely deny the specificity and nature of relations, which is that they connect terms directly, without the need for other connections, conceiving them as another kind of term[13] Only under these conditions can one demand from relations what is instead peculiar to terms. It is as if there could be a country whose judicial system did not provide for any final degree of judgement and any and all judgements could always be appealed. This would effectively amount to the absence of judicial power.

---

13 This interpretation can be found in Bradley's text, cf. *Appearance* and *Reality,* p. 33. Later, when he elaborated the theory of logical types, Russell gave a new and more articulate version. of the inadequacy of any conception of relations as a 'third term between the other two'. This error would arise from the fact that the words that stand for relations are just as substantial as those that stand for terms, while the relationship to their respective meanings is of a different kind bend common language is unable to express this difference. In an ideal language, the respect of the logical types would be entrusted to the form, which rather than expressing the differences would exhibit them_ So, for example, to exhibit the relation "under" in "A is under B" we would have to write the sign "A" under the sign "B".

It is the terms that need relations to connect each other, not the relations themselves. The relations connect, the terms are connected. The very example given by Bradley, that of the chain[14] should have warned against such confusion. "If his argument had been valid," Russell observes, "it would have resulted in the impossibility of chains, which in fact do exist". The successive links are not joined by links but by an external relation that does not require any other relation to fulfil its office.[15]

The monist thesis was also exposed to a further and independent objection. Russell admits the existence of a regress but denies it specific refutative validity. That is, he admits that a relation connecting two terms is itself in relation to each term, and that this relation too has in turn to be connected to the first by another relation, and so on. In this process we must, however, distinguish two kinds of regress:

> the one proceeding merely to perpetually new implied propositions, the other in the meaning of a proposition itself; of these two kinds we agreed that the former since the solution of the problem of infinity has ceased to be objectionable, while the latter remains inadmissible.[16]

In other words, it is necessary to distinguish the two aspects of implication and analysis, or rather, an infinite process of implication from an infinite process of analysis; if, by saying that in order for a relation to connect terms it must itself be connected to terms, we mean a sort of prerequisite that allows the relation to be established and in the absence of which it is not necessary, in a temporal or conditional vision, the regress that is generated is unacceptable because the concept of relation presupposes (assuming it) relationality itself and therefore is vitiated by circularity. If, on the contrary, we understand that a given relation between two terms implies relationality, that is, if we state that a concept implies itself the regress implied here is neither vicious nor circular. It is not, in fact, part of the meaning of the

---

14   F. H. Bradley, *Appearance and Reality,* pp. 31-33.
15   B.Russell, *An Outline of Philosophy,* p.263
16   B.Russell, *The Principles of Mathematics,* p.99.

proposition; it is not part of the meaning of a relational proposition to assert a relation between the relation and its terms.

From the distinction of the two types of regress and the demonstration that the one, implicit in relational propositions, is logically admissible again follows, according to Russell, what he calls their 'absolute and metaphysical validity'.

The thesis against which the Russellian criticism of monism was particularly tenacious is that of the characterisation of relations as properties not of the terms taken individually but of the whole that they compose. Perhaps Bradley would not willingly accept this reading of his doctrine; he would certainly have seen in it a distributive conception of the Whole that he rejected.

In stating that relations characterise units, he did not in fact intend to argue only that they would be impossible outside a totality, but also that this totality could not conceive of itself as the sum of its parts. The very notion of parts was a concern for his conception of reality and still fell into the limbo of appearance. The Whole is in fact. as we have seen, at the same time the parts and their transcendence.

This view implied, at any rate, that if A and B are close, it is the whole (AB) that is characterised by the relation of proximity. But if such a conception is, to some extent. compatible with symmetrical relations such as proximity, i.e. with those relations that proceed both from the *referent* to the *relatum* and the other way, it could in no way be considered adequate for asymmetrical relations.

Asymmetrical relations are those that proceed from one term to the other but not the reverse; for example, the relations "father"; "greater than"; "left of" etc. are asymmetrical. If we try to reduce the relation "A is greater than B" to a property of the complex (AB), the meaning of the original proposition will be irretrievably lost, because the statement that the complex (AB) is characterised by the relation "greater" does not allow us to distinguish the direction of the relation, the antecedent from the consequent, that is, it does not allow us to know whether A is greater than B or B is greater than A. The complex (AB) and the complex (BA) are in fact formed by the same components and the only distinguishing characteristic is precisely the direction of the relation, which in this case proceeds from A to B and not vice versa. According to Russell, the monist theory is unable to preserve this difference and thus to preserve the meaning of relational propositions. [17]

On the affirmation of external relations Russell based his pluralist ontology. But,we need to ask, what is the connection between relation theory and ontology, between the assertion that relations are ultimate components of the world, are irreducible to properties, and finally between the assertion of external relations and pluralism.

First of all, it can be observed that if the subject-predicate form is the one to which all propositions can be reduced and if language reflects reality, every fact must consist of a substance and an attribute. The assertion of a plurality of substances expressed, for example, by the proposition "The world consists of a multiplicity of objects and events" cannot be subsumed under this form. Propositions containing numbers or asserting a plurality of entities are not reducible to several subject-predicate propositions because the number or plurality results from the one proposition and would be lost in a set of propositions each asserting a unity. If, therefore, propositions asserting a plurality are legitimate propositions of our language and are not reducible to the subject-predicate form, it follows that the latter is not the only possible form and with its uniqueness the monism connected with it falls away. [18]

Then, to this argument, i.e. the rigidly referential conception of meaning that Russell held at the time he wrote *The Principles of Mathematics* is grafted this conclusion. In order to have meaning, linguistic expressions must denote non-linguistic entities, and these entities constitute their meaning. Now since there are in our language signifying propositions containing relational expressions these expressions must denote entities. These entities, while not having the same ontological *status* as objects that can be experienced with the senses, have, as universals, a different form of being. They "subsist" rather than "exist" according to the distinction advanced by Meinong in his 1913 essay *Über Gegenstandtsheorie* that two

---

17 On the issue related to the *direction* of relations and in general on asymmetrical relations see B. Russell, *The Principles of Mathematics,* pp. 227 ff.

18 *The Philosophy of Leibniz,* p.12.

years later Russell himself would reject, (together with *unicorns* and *golden mountains*) but this different forms of being do not take away their characteristic as ultimate components of the world.[19]

The logical fallacy of the doctrine of internal relations as the foundation and presupposition of monism constitutes, therefore, the incentive for Russell's elaboration of his own theory of "external relations" and the explication of that pluralistic demand that will be satisfied in the *Principia* through a rigorously extensional formulation of the logic of relations in whose terms, as with those of the logic of classes, it will be possible to express mathematics.

The pluralistic horizon of Russell's theory of external relations thus qualifies on a specific philosophical ground the attempt of the *Principia* to lead mathematics back to logic, and supports the work of assimilation and deepening of the results that Peano and Frege had already begun in the field of number theory, successions and ordinal and cardinal arithmetic. [20]

---

19   A comprehensive discussion on Meinong treatment of these entities may be found in ; Swanson, Carolyn. *Reburial of nonexistents reconsidering the Meinong-Russell debate*, Amsterdam ; New York: Rodopi, 2011,

20   In this regard, it may be interesting to note that Russell had already published, in Peano's notation, his first article on relations entitled 'The Logic of Relations' in the *Journal of Mathematics,* 7, 1900-1901, pp. 115-148 reprinted later in *Logic and Knowledge.*

CHAPTER FOUR
CONSTRUCTIONISM AND
LOGICAL ATOMISM

Russell's pluralist ontology rests, as we have seen, on the theory of external relations; this position will result, as is well known, in what is unanimously considered the most significant theoretical contribution of his thought, *logical atomism*, the most salient feature of which lies in the original link connecting, in this theory logical analysis and metaphysics. At this point it is necessary to show how the logical theory in general and that of logical constructionism in particular underlies as a metaphysical vision – partly overt but partly concealed – his logical atomism, into which it will flow and of which it constitutes the preparatory phases. The doctrine of logical atomism will not be examined, here in detail; Only those aspects will be illustrated that differentiate Russell's atomistic analysis from that of other philosophers, primarily Ludwig Wittgenstein. We'll try to highlight how the subsequent overcoming of his own philosophical vision can be traced back to Russell himself, who, with his radical and sometime scorching intellectual rigour once said that he preferred infanticide to the sacrifice of truth, so that he himself was to be the first to highlight its major difficulties.

Despite the variety of problems at stake and the many solutions proposed, Russell's philosophy is pervaded by a methodological drive that runs through all his intellectual life. His researches all show, in fact, the will to introduce into the examination of philosophical problems the rigour and clarity typical of the more advanced and exact sciences such as mathematics and logic. The interest that he nurtured in logic, of which he can be considered one of the most qualified reformers, did not, however, exhaust itself in the investigation of the peculiar problems of that discipline, but took on an important functional character in the examination and treatment of general problems in the theory of knowledge.

In this sense, the most significant moment in his philosophical research, the one in which the need for rigour and the urgency of the most radical problems come together in an organic expression, is undoubtedly to be found in *logical atomism*, a theory in which perhaps the two most important contributions to its final formulation culminate: the theory of descriptions and the constructionism. In effect, these two expressions, in addition to referring to certain theories, which can be precisely dated, designate a multiplicity of problems and researches that Russell, starting at least from 1897[1], developed respectively on the logical and epistemological level and that would lead him, after a long critical work, to the complex and organic system of logical atomism, as expressed in the later lectures of 1918[2], in which the fundamental influence exerted on him by the young Wittgenstein[3]plays, as it is well-known an extremely important role.

---

1   To this year dates Russell's first work *An Essay on the Foundations of Geometry* (Cambridge: Cambridge Univ. Press,)

2   *The Philosophy of Logical Atomism,* in *Logic and Knowledge,* pp. 105-246, which collects the text of the eight 1918 London lectures delivered in Gordon Square (and possibly attended also by some of his friends members of the so called *Bloomsbury Group*) published in *The Monist* between 1918 and 1919.

3   Logical atomism is in fact linked above all to the Russell-Wittgenstein pairing, even if many divergences characterise the two philosophers. As far as the time span of this enquiry overlaps Wittgenstein's philosophical development we recall that the first most complete formulation of his thought is to be found in the *Tractatus Logico-philosophicus* (London: Routledge & Kegan Paul 1922, edited by C. A. Ogden and F. P. Ramsey. A new translation is that edited by D. F. Pears and B. F. McGuinness, ibid., 1961; It goes without saying that the subsequent developments of Wittgenstein's philosophy centred on his *Phillophische Bemerkungen* are beyond the span of this study and are therefore not taken into account. The comparative critical research and literature on the two philosophers' thought, is overwhelming. For some now classical studies see James. O. Urmson, *Philosophical Analysis* (Oxford: Oxford University Press, 1956), J. Griffin, *Wittgenstein's Logical Atomism* (Oxford: Oxford University Press, 1964); J. Feibleman, *Inside the Great Mirror. A Critical*

We need, therefore, not only to drew the attention to the network of topics and researches that go under the two labels of "doctrine of descriptions" and "constructionist theory of knowledge" but, above all, identify in this dual, logical and epistemological direction of Russell's early investigations the preparatory stages of the formulation of his Atomism.

When, in 1905, Russell published the essay that constitutes the original drafting of the theory of descriptions[4] expressed five years later in the first volume of the *Principia Mathematica,* he had behind him some important works on the foundations of geometry and mathematics as well as a work on Leibnitz whose metaphysics, not by chance, stimulated the interest of the future author of logical atomism from then on. The subject matter of Russell's early mathematical essays would, as is well known, flow into the three constituent volumes of the *Principia,* in a more mature and substantially definitive version. In our discussion we shall not refer to it except insofar as we need to gradually gather both from *Principles of Mathematics,* and from other minor essays, the elements of that new interpretation of relations that constitutes the most relevant philosophical acquisition of Russell's first production..

The logic of relations is, however, only one part of the great building of the *Principia,* and of the system's logical-mathematical apparatus. As much important as Russell's contribution to its construction are the efforts to clarify the philosophical reflections of this new conceptual instrument of Alfred N. Whitehead on the one hand and of George Moore on the other who collaborated to an even greater extent in the clarification of all the problems at stake.[5] Where Russell's contribution proves to be unquestionably of primary importance is in the elaboration that in the logic of the

---

Exposition of the Philosophy of B. Russell, L. Wittgenstein and their Followers (The Hague: Martinus Nijhoff, 1958)

4   *On Denoting* Mind, XIV, 1905, pp. 473-493, reprinted in *Logic and knowledge* pp. 39-56

5   Cf.. in this respect Whitehead's contribution in *Principia* or as indicated by Russell himself in "Whitehead and Principia Mathematica", in *Mind,* 57, 1948, pp. 137 ff. and G. E. Moore's, 'External and Internal Relations', in *Proceedings of the Aristotelian Society,* 1919-20, pp. 40-62.

Principia precedes that of classes. The theoretical premise of the logic of classes is in fact that theory of descriptions that remains one of the creations of Russell's speculative genius, "That paradigm of Philosophy", as Frank Ramsey defined it in 1929[6].

The theory of descriptions, along with that of external relations examined earlier, will in fact prove to be strictly connected to Russell's constructionist conception of epistemology, as expressed in works thematically and chronologically close to the elaboration of propositions as descriptive functions. The theory of descriptions was first fully published by Russell in the article On *Denoting*[7] in which. rejecting both Meinong's views on negative existents and the Fregean distinction of sense and meaning,[8] he judged incorrect the assumption that in a meaningful utterance each of its components has a meaning even if taken in isolation; that is, that it has its own ontological correspondence. Russell distinguished two types of symbols, *simple* and *complex* ones: names and descriptions The core of the distinction is that names. unlike descriptions, directly *denote* an object and this object is their meaning. While the apprehension of a proper name is linked to the experience of the object it signifies[9] the apprehension of sentences is linked to the knowledge of the individual components. Descriptions, on the other hand, are complex symbols, composed of other simple symbols, i.e. they are 'apparent names'. The sentence 'the author of Waverley', a now classic example, is a description, i.e. a complex symbol composed of the words 'author', 'Waverley', article and prepositions. Descriptions, Russell argues, have no meaning when taken in isolation, even if they contribute to

---

6   Cf. *The Foundations of Mathematics, and other Essay* (London: Routledge & Kegan Paul, 1931) p. 263n

7   For a complete view of Russell's treatment of this subject see *Introduction to Philosophy of Mathematics*, ch. XVI; *The Problems of Philosophy ch.* V. On this topic, cf. the work of G.E.. Moore, *Russell's Theory Cf. Descriptions,* in P.A. Schilpp, *ed. The Philosophy of B.R.,* pp. 177-225 and P. A. Geach, *Russell's Theory of Descriptions,* "Analysis", X, 3, 1950, pp. 84-88; L.Linsky. *Referring,* London 1967, chapters III, IV, V; V. Quine, "On what there is" in *From a Logical Point of view,* Cambridge, Mass.: Harvard University Press 1951).

8   In *Logic and Arithmetic, cit.,* pp. 374-404- See also footnote 38 n Ch. 3

9   'The Philosophy of Logical Atomism', cit. p. 246.

the meaning of the context in which they occur. Russell's analysis of these utterances leads to the distinction between grammatical and logical subjects and to the elimination of the former when they do not match with the latter. Judgments containing descriptions are analysed by replacing the grammatical subject with a quantification variable (one, some, all) and changing propositions into enunciative functions.[10]

Russell attributed to Meinong, perhaps misrepresenting his thinking, the belief that every grammatical subject is a denotating expression corresponding to an object[11]. "The present King of France" or "The Golden Mountain" would, according to this theory, have some sort of existence or being, in the sense that their reference is in the mind of the thinker. This seemed to Russell not only contrary to the sense of reality always invoked but also to the principle of non-contradiction. Even though Frege had already overcome this difficulty by distinguishing the two aspects of meaning and denotation, new difficulties arose in relation to utterances that, although they have meaning, lack denotation, such as "The King of France is bald", which for Russell is a false utterance rather than meaningless. The only solution seemed to him to abandon "the view that denotation is what it is all about in judgements containing denotative phrases". [12]

In the now classic example 'Scott is the author of Waverley' Russell notes that this judgement expresses an identity of denotation in the sense that both the name 'Scott' and the description 'the author of Waverley' refer to the same person. Logically speaking, according to the law of the indiscernibility of identicals, they should,

---

10 Given the general character of this work, which is mainly aimed at the study of the general philosophical presuppositions of Russell's thought, the albeit very interesting subject of descriptions is not explored here, except insofar as it serves the primary purposes of the investigation. An interesting collection of essays on this subject can be found in Reimer, M. and A. Bezuidenhout, *Descriptions and Beyond*, Oxford, New York, Oxford University press, 2004

11 Cf. Or *Denoting*, p. 45 and "Knowledge by Acquaintance and Knowledge by Description", pp. 108-128,

12 *On Denoting*. p. 46 ff. For a recent contextualist reading of Meinong's view see ; Carolyn. Swanson ;, *Reburial of nonexistents reconsidering the Meinong-Russell debate* (Amsterdam; New York, NY: Rodopi, 2011)

therefore, be mutually substitutable *salva veritate*. But "Scott is the author of Waverley" is not equivalent to "Scott is Scott" because in the latter case, unlike the former, we have a tautology devoid of any informative value. The description is in fact a misnomer and therein lies its informational value; while its impossibility of being replaced by a proper name lies in its lack of ontological reference. Russell's analysis resolves the difficulty by replacing grammatical subjects with variables and leads to the elimination of the phrase "the author of Waverley" which by itself means neither Scott nor anything else. The theory of descriptions was the subject of a controversy between Russell and Strawson. The latter refuted Russell's analysis in the article "On Referring", introducing the concepts of "use" and "mention" of utterances and expressions. He appealed to what were to be known as 'incomplete description'. Russell replied to this writing with the article *Mr Strawson or Reference*,[13] Description, as such, while contributing to the meaning of the proposition in which it occurs, taken in isolation has no meaning. The debate was to go on for more than fifty years, focused mainly on the *referential / attributive* distinction.[14]

For Russell, words and even proper names were sometimes descriptions, and to have highlighted their character as incomplete symbols was a fundamental discovery not only for logic but also, as we shall see, for the theory of knowledge. For him, all our knowledge is in fact inevitably led to the things of which we have direct knowledge, "every proposition that we are able to understand", he

---

13   Cf. *My Philosophical Development,* p. 63-4; *Mind,* X, LIX, 1950, pp. 320-44, *cit.* For a more detailed examination of the problem of reference, C. E Caton, Strawson on "Referring" in *Mind,* X, 68, 1959, hp. 539-44; P. Geach, *Reference and Generality* Ithaca, 1962; L Linsky, *Reference and Referents,* in C. E. Caton (ed.) *Philosophv and Ordinary Language,* Urbana, 1963 and *Referring,* dr.; J. Searle, 'Proper Names' in *Mind.* X, LXVII, 1958, pp. 166-73; V. V. O. Quine. "On what there is", in *From a Logical point of view.* and *World and object,* Cambridge, Mass., 1960.

14   A more recent interesting recollection of this debate may be found in, *Descriptions and Beyond,* edited by Marga Reimer and Anne Bezuidenhout (Oxford, New York, Oxford University Press, 2004) see in particular the essays by F. Recanati and Ernie Lepore)

writes in the *Problems of Philosophy*, "must be composed entirely of terms of which we have direct knowledge."[15]

Russell's epistemology, which is rigorously analytical, is in fact characterised, on the one hand, by research into the nature of the relationship between subject and object namely knowledge and, on the other, by the attempt to specify the terms of this relationship. This analysis should lead to the identification of the irreducible components of the world with a methodology that is free both from psychologistic integrations and from unjustified inferences. This research, in which logical analysis becomes an instrument of ontology, constitutes a further step towards the later conceptions of atomism into which it will flow, and already heralds, in the distinction between two types of knowledge and in the image on the verifiability of physics that we will refer to, the thesis of the structural isomorphism between world and logic on which the entire atomistic theme is centred.

It is well known that Russell provided different and sometimes conflicting versions of his worldview and of the ways and limits of human knowledge. However, two main moments can be distinguished in his thought. Until 1914 he advocated a realist and dualist theory; in the years between 1914 and 1958 he put forward the constructionist doctrine that we shall now examine until he embraced, after 1921, the theses of James and the American behaviourist psychologists, known as neutral monism.

We will not offer here a detailed examination of Russell's epistemology, but shall only draw the attention within the proposed tripartition to the aspects most directly connected to the atomistic view. Russellian dualism of the early period is characterised by the conception of knowledge as a connection between two irreducible terms: the subject and the object, one of which is mental and the other material. He also distinguished this relationship into knowledge by learning *(knowledge by acquaintance)* and *knowledge by description*. Knowledge by learning, which he also called direct knowledge, cannot be distinguished into true and false since truth

---

15 Cf. *The Problems of Philosophy* (Oxford: Oxford University press, published as E book 2001 p. 39 the quotation is from this edition.

and falsehood pertain to language or rather to the correspondence between language and fact. By learning, i.e. directly, we know our sensory data while the objects that correspond to them we only know by description. In introspection we have direct experience of feelings, volitions, thoughts and, through memory, of objects of which we have had immediate experience in the past[16] Russell in *Problems* admitted, but uncertainly, that we also have some experience of the self. In perception we are aware not only of the data; but also of our awareness. (*Ibid.,* pp. 58-60) [17]

The transition to logical constructionism can be traced, in Russell's chronology, around 1914, the year in which the texts of some of his lectures given in March-April in Boston where published[18] together with other of his essays on the relation between common sense and scientific knowledge, later collected in a volume.[19]

Constructivist epistemology was intended by its author to solve the difficulties of a radically empiricist conception of knowledge that had remained largely unresolved in the *Problems.* Russell was primarily concerned with resolving the contrast that arose between science and philosophy within the empiricist theory of knowledge, according to which all knowledge comes from the senses. This problem, which was particularly relevant in the case of physics, whose concepts seemed irreducible to sense data, led him in his essay *The Relation of Sense Data to Physics* (Ibid.) to considerably modify the terms of his dualism. In order to validly ground physics from an empiricist point of view, it was necessary that its supposed contents of the material world (atoms, molecules., electrons, etc.) could relate to the sense data from which the cognitive process begins for empiricists, their truth being beyond doubt.

This correlation appeared very problematic to him since of its two terms (datum – physical concepts) only one is known, namely the

---

16   Cf.. *The Problems of Philosophy* pp-.34-41
17   These items were taken up in many other works including *Our Knowledge of the External World, ch.* III; *The Analysis of Mind, Meaning and Truth, ch.* VII; *Human Knowledge*, part I, ch. VII and part II, ch. IV.
18   *Our Knowledge of the external world,*
19   *Mysticism and logic, cit.*

sensible datum, which is quite different from the particles into which physicists break down matter[20].

The search for a well-grounded empirical verifiability of physics will lead Russell to overturn the traditional approach according to which sensory data are functions of physical objects, leading him to affirm instead that the objects of physics and those of common sense are functions of sensory data[21] and must therefore be described and conceived in terms of data. In short, this is the general theory of physics and constructionist epistemology, characterised by the application of 'Ockam's razor' and the inversion of the traditional inference from data back to matter, according to a procedure we will briefly sketch. Alongside sensory data, Russell introduced a new epistemological category: the *sensibilia*. They were given the same status as data but differed from them in that they were not really perceived by anyone.[22] Assuming a Leibnizian-type universe, he resolved objects into the set of possible points of view; into the 'class of their appearances regardless of whether or not they are given'[23] to any percipient subject. This design that already presents the characteristic traits of atomism is that of "reconstructing the conception of matter without the a priori beliefs that have historically originated it".*(Ibid.*,p.111) offering an explanation that, while not denying its metaphysical reality, did not affirm it either, thus avoiding the inference of common sense that from the relative permanence and stability of data goes back to the existence of permanent matter, identifying what is real with what is permanent. Common sense in tracing back from appearances to the 'thing' was, in his view, gratuitous metaphysics. (*Ibid.,* p.112) As far as both common sense and the laws of physics are concerned, the appearances that are the only certain data, perform the same functions as the 'thing', and the criteria of continuity and causal laws that apply to things can

---

20   Cf. *Our Knowledge of the External World,* ch. IV and *The Relation of Sense Data to Physics,* in *Mysticism and Logic,* ch. VIII.
21   *Our knowledge of the External World,* p. 72 ff.
22   *'The Relation of Sense Data to Physics',* pp. 148-50.
23   Cf. *Our Knowledge of the External World,* pp. 109-110,25

with equal result apply to appearances. The multiplication of entities therefore did not appear necessary.[24]

Just as the 'thing' was resolved in the series of its appearances, the self – the other term of dualism and of the cognitive relationship – was also losing its stable ontological status with the application of constructionism. In the essay "On the nature of acquaintance" Russell defined *acquaintance* as a relationship between an experienced object and an experiencing subject, but no longer argued for the absolute possibility of knowing the subject independently of that experience and outside the relation called *acquaintance*. The establishment of an identity between subjects of different experiences seemed to him an inference to be rejected because it was not susceptible of demonstration. He therefore asserted that the experience of the self is always linked to our consciousness of a given relation of which we are aware, i.e. that "we can easily be conscious of our experiences, but we never seem to be conscious of the subject itself"[25]. The ultimate residue of knowledge was identified precisely in that relationship *(acquaintance)* that exists between intrinsically unknowable terms, whose ontological status escapes us completely. He therefore limited himself to stating that 'when we have known that an experience is constituted by the relation called *acquaintance* we can define the self as the subject of the actual experience'.(ibid. P. 165)

By the beginning of 1921, Russell definitely abandoned dualism and embraced the monist theses advocated by James. The acceptance of this philosophical view characterised by the abandonment of the subject-object distinction, in Russell's thought, appears as the natural outcome of a strict application of constructionism. When he started to apply this method of investigation to the analysis of mental processes, he came to the conclusion that mind, as well as matter, is also a logical construction. He therefore argued that

> if we are to avoid a perfectly gratuitous assumption, we must dispense the conception that the subject as one of the actual ingredients

---

24 'The relation between sense data and physics', in *Mysticism and Logic,* pp. 146-7.

25 *On the Nature of Acquaintance* 162-3

of the world[26] […] and that I think the person is not an ingredient in the single thought: he is rather constituted by relations of the thoughts to each other and to the body. (*ibid.*, pp. 17-18)

In this way, any *fundamentum divisionis* was missing.

With the distinction between subject and object, the distinction between sensation and sensory data also necessarily fell, and Russell could thus claim that the only substance *(stuff)* of which the world is made up are 'sensations' and 'images', which as such are neither physical nor mental. It is only the imperfection of our language that leads us to this mistaken belief by hypostatising what are merely ways of associating sensations and images. Russellian neutral monism, however, differs, as has already been observed[27], from that of James and the behaviourists, since Russell reintroduces a certain dualism. While affirming the neutrality of the components of the world, he upholds the dualism of causal laws. This dualism implies that the particulars, i.e. sensations and images are connected according to different laws. Sensations are subject as much to physical laws, such as gravitation, as to the laws of psychology, such as association, and are therefore totally neutral, while images connect only according to psychological laws[28.] However, we are interested to note that the basis of monism is, as we shall see, an atomistic metaphysics, founded on the independence of particulars.

Logical atomism represents the most systematic expression of Russell's philosophy, in which the complex and rigorous articulation of logical theories and analyses reveals most clearly the general metaphysical design that underlies them and constitutes their theoretical framework.

26　*The Analysis of Mind*, p. 142.

27　M. Weitz, "Analysis and the Unity of Russell's Philosophy" in P.A. Schilpp (ed.), *The Philosophy of Bertrand Russell,* pp. 55-121. For a critical view of this aspect of Russell's philosophy see also J. Laird, "On certain Russell's views concerning the human mind" in P. A. Schilpp, *The Philosophy of Bertrand Russell,* pp. 293-316 and P. A. Ushenko, "Russell's critique of empiricism", ibid., pp. 385-418; W. Stace, "Russell's neutral monism", ibid., pp. 351-385, as well as Russell's responses to the criticism on pp. 698-700 and 706-710 of the same volume.

28　*The Analysis of Mind,* pp. 25-26.

Only a rather, sketchy exposition of Russell atomism and a general outline of his fundamental theses will follow.. It will thus be possible, on the one hand, to make explicit the close link that connects, in Russell's thought, the logical and metaphysical themes and, on the other, to make more evident the confluence in logical atomism of both the elements of his pre-1914 philosophy and the following constructionist turn. In this examination we refer above all to the eight lectures that Russell delivered at Gordon Square in London in 1918 later published in the *Monist,* which seem the most complete formulation of his thought.

With his analysis, Russell wanted to give, on the one hand, a view of the world and provide, on the other, the tools for further research to be pursued with those guarantees of rigour customary in scientific research.

It is well known that in those years Russell took up Wittgenstein's ideas to a considerable extent. a debt that he openly acknowledged in *The Philosophy of Logical Atomism* and to which we refer. Since the very first lecture on atomism, reappears the pluralistic instance, which, starting from the theory of descriptions and the constructionist epistemology, had characterised the course of his theoretical approach: according to the atomist *weltanschauung,* the world is made up of an indefinite number of elementary facts, independent of one another, which can combine into complexes, lacking a stiff own ontological *status* apart from the elementary or atomic facts of which they are composed. Russell's pluralism is here reformulated through the statement of the mutual independence of facts. Knowledge of the world is first conceived as knowledge of all atomic facts, which are traced back by the analysis of the complexes. The foundation of atomist epistemology rests, as can be seen from the second of the above-mentioned lectures, on the assumptions that the ontological complexity of the world is mirrored by logic;[29] which amounts to a structural isomorphism between (ideal) language and the world. The elementary facts would correspond to the elementary or atomic propositions, which are also mutually independent of each other on

---

29   "The Philosophy of Logical Atomism", cit., p. 197.

a logical level and can also be combined into complex propositions, which are susceptible to reductive analysis. (ibidem p. 189 ff)

At this point, it should be clear our initial assumption that the theory of relations, the theory of descriptions, and the theory of types constitute together with the constructionism method the scaffolding of the global vision of Russell's atomism. This will become even clearer when we consider that the mirror-image relationship posited by Russell between logical order and ontological order is not between common language and world but between logical analysed language and world. The structure of natural languages in fact, their syntax and grammar are far from the rigorous precision of logic, so that instead of acting as a cognitive tool, they often conceal, hide reality, giving rise to mistakes and false unreliable beliefs (*Ibid.,* p. 241 ff.). In this thesis, the influence exerted by Wittgenstein on Russell's conception of language appears in all its clarity: the philosopher's task is logical analysis, that is, the work aimed at creating a rigorous language that – analysed in all its parts depicts – on the assumption of the isomorphic relationship – the ontological structure of reality.

The whole Russellian procedure, as is clear, makes use of the logical tools developed in the preceding years from the *Principles of Mathematics*, and the analysis constitutes, as has also been pointed out, a continuous attempt at definition on two levels: on the level of the real in the sense of seeking and enumerating all the properties of a given non-linguistic complex and independently of our use of symbolism (i.e. language), and on the linguistic level in the sense of defining the appropriate contextual use of this symbolism. so as not to give rise to paradoxes, i.e. not to be ontologically misleading.[30]

Russell made his programme clear from the very first of the eight lectures, showing his intention to illustrate 'a certain kind of logical theory and, on the basis of this, a certain kind of metaphysics'. And specifying that 'the reason why he called his doctrine logical atomism was because the atoms he wished to arrive at as the last residue of analysis were logical and not physical atoms'.[31] In other words, he proposed an investigation aimed at 'determining the simple entities

---

30   See M. Weitz, pp. 110-121.
31   "The Philosophy of Logical Atomism", pp. 178-179.

of language that correspond to the structure of reality and that also constitute the foundations of knowledge'[32] pointing out an approach whose intuition dates back to the early years of the century.

For the purpose of the continuity and connections of the elements of Russell's speculation, it should be recalled that the analysis of descriptions as incomplete symbols, i.e. linguistic entities lacking ontological reference -which forms the subject of the Sixth Lecture on Logical Atomism – is of primary importance in this system, It had been formulated, as we have seen, as early as 1905 and represented the general approach of philosophical research with the instruments of logic. The adoption of the analytical epistemological perspective was also present in *Our Knowledge of the External World* and particularly in the second essay: 'Logic as the Essence of Philosophy'. That essay stated that

> every philosophical problem when subjected to analysis and the necessary purification process appears logical or not really philosophical (p. 42).

Thus, the fundamental theses of the extensionality and structural isomorphism of world and logic clearly converge in the methodology of logical atomism, and the previously elaborated techniques of analysis reveal their underlying metaphysical design..

We will now attempt to outline the development of atomistic analysis by focusing on what we consider its core, namely the general theory of atomic facts. A fact, according to Russell, is not a thing but a 'state of things' that are the irreducible simple elements [33] This difference between facts and things corresponds to the linguistic difference between propositions and nouns.

> When I speak of a fact, Russell stated as early as 1914, I do not mean one of the simple things that are in the world, but rather I mean

---

32 Cf. P. Filiasi Carcano, *Introduzione alla lettura del 'Tractatus' di Wittgenstein*, Rome, s.e. 1966, pp. 56-57.

33 Russell's *things* are not the objects of common sense, but *particulars* like perceptions, sensations.

a certain thing that has a certain quality or certain things that have a certain relation.[34]

It is the kind of thing that makes a proposition true or false",[35]whereas the ultimate components of facts are those entities that Russell called "the particulars"[36].

Analysis takes place from facts and not from things because it is the former that constitute the world by combining with each other, while things, considered in themselves, determine nothing outside the complexes in which they are found.

> Just as in the study of chess, Ramsey comments, nothing is gained by talking about the atoms of which the pieces are composed, so in the study of logic nothing is gained by entering into the ultimate analysis of names and the objects they signify.[37]

Although the ideal of atomism was that of an extensional construction of both facts and propositions, from atomic facts and propositions, Russell recognised two types of ultimate facts, i.e. irreducible to other facts. He defined as "atomic" or "particular" those facts that consist in the possession of a quality by a thing as in the proposition "this is white". Other atomic facts are those consisting in the relations between two or more terms. The set of atomic facts, reflected in the set of atomic propositions, should constitute an "inventory of the world". We shall see later, however, that Russell makes some exceptions to this interpretation.

Linguistic analysis revealed that propositions, like facts, are complexes, and that among their components are those expressed linguistically by verbs and predicates, i.e. relations and qualities.[38] Such qualities are inherent in and subsist between terms that are the logical subjects of propositions i.e. what Russell calls the particulars. (*Ibid.,* p. 200).

---

34   Cf. Our *Knowledge of the External World,* cit., p. 61.
35   "The Philosophy of Logical Atomism", cit., p. 182.
36   Cf. G. Bergmann, "Russell on Particulars", *in Philosophical Review,* 1947, reprinted in *The Metaphysics of Logical Positivism.* London 1954.
37   Cf. F.P. Ramsey, "Facts and Propositions", p. 162
38   Cf. "The Philosophy of Logical Atomism", p. 197.

The atomists, and foremost among them Wittgenstein, called the relation of correspondence that links facts to language "representation" or "picture". This connection is configured in the relation called *meaning* to which the analyses of logical atomism are largely dedicated, and in which the investigations on language that Russell had begun with the *Principles* converge. It is easy to understand, also in the light of the work of Frege and Meinong, as well as in the isomorphic presupposition the importance of the rigorous determination of the relation of meaning on which the entire conception of language as symbolism is centred, and to which he dedicates the sixth and seventh lectures on atomism. It is a great Russell's achievement the elucidation of complexity of this relation, that he made explicit since his earliest writings and whose analysis he continued to deepen.

The fundamental distinction he made is that between the way of meaning of propositions and that of nouns. "The relation that a proposition can have to a fact," Russell points out, "is essentially of two kinds: that which has a true proposition and that which has a false proposition". (*Ibid.,* p. 187). Both refer to the same fact, Since the dualism of true and false does not affect facts (which as such are neither true nor false) but only propositions. They are not "names of facts" but "complex symbols", the complexity of which consists in being made up of words that can also occur individually in other signifying propositions. It is perhaps worth mentioning that Russell uses 'proposition' in the sense of 'utterance', propositions, which assert or deny something [39]similar to the Aristotelian apophantic discourse but with the fundamental difference of not being restricted to the subject-predicate form.

Propositions, as we have seen, do not 'name' facts: he conceived naming as a univocal relation binding the thing to its name, in the sense that the name that does not "correspond" or refer to the particular named, does not "signify" or "mean" it, and ceases to be a name remaining a simple noise, whereas "a proposition does not cease to be a proposition when it is false"[40].If we analyse a judgement

---

39   Cf. *Our Knowledge of the External World,* p. 163.
40   "The Philosophy of Logical Atomism", pp. 187-188.

such as "Socrates is mortal" it becomes clear, says Russell, that "Socrates" means a certain man, the word "mortal" means a certain quality, and the utterance "Socrates is mortal" means a certain fact, and that these three kinds of meaning are quite distinct, and one will fall into the most inextricable contradictions if one thinks that the word "meaning" has the same meaning in each of these three cases" (*Ibid.*, pp. 186-187). [41]

As well as its promoter, Russell ended to become the harshest critic of logical atomism of which he denounced many theoretical difficulties that he tried to overcome with solutions not always shared by other philosophical analysts and atomists.

A rigorous conception of atomism forbade the recognition of facts other than atomic ones, on the basis of the extensional constitution of language, i.e. the total reducibility of complex or molecular propositions to elementary ones: Russell was nonetheless the only atomist philosopher to admit with valid arguments the untenability of a rigorous atomism, indirectly opening the way to the revolt against atomism that would lead to the "Oxford Philosophy", which, abandoning the perspective of a radical reductionism, would turn towards a descriptive and contextual analysis of ordinary language inspired above all by Wittgenstein's *Philosophische Untersuchungen.* [42]

It is no coincidence that a large part of the eight lectures consists of an examination of the difficulties encountered by a rigid atomist conception. The English philosopher had to admit, alongside atomic facts, the existence of other types of equally irreducible facts, such as *general* facts, *negative* facts and facts corresponding to *intentional* constructs. This recognition, which upset the entire atomist theory, arose from the impossibility of explaining so-called general propositions, negative propositions and intentional constructs within the framework of a true-functional language.

Of particular importance in this respect is the analysis of intensional propositions. A complex (molecular) disjunctive proposition of the

---

41 Russell treated the problems of meaning again but from a behaviourist point of view in *Meaning and Truth,* and in *Human Knowledge*
42 Oxford, 1953

type "pVq" does not postulate a new type of disjunctive fact in addition to the atomic ones in order to be explained, but rather refers to two facts corresponding to "p" and "q" respectively. Propositions expressing beliefs or judgements (such as "A believes p") cannot be regarded as truth-functions of the atomic ones for Russell. In the example "A believes p", "p" seems to enter into the complex proposition not only with its truth-value but with its whole content; the truth of the complex proposition does not in this case depend on the truth or falsity of "p", in the sense that the substitution of "p" for another of the same truth-value would alter the complex proposition. Already in the *Principia*[43] Russell had considered such constructs 'intentional functions'. In 1918 he discussed and rejected the behaviourist analysis according to which "A believes p" is to be interpreted as meaning that A behaves in such and such a way, that not the proposition "p" but the words "p" are the elements of the fact. A view that he later accepted *in the Analysis of Mind*[44] In 1918 he tried instead to save the true-functional thesis, threatened by such propositions by advancing the hypothesis that beliefs were irreducible special facts[45]. This version of his, which was of course not accepted by the other atomist philosophers[46] left the problem substantially open, and Wittgenstein. offered a solution on the true-functional level, according to which "A believes p" was analysed in A believes the proposition and the proposition, if true, says the fact (A believes "p" and "p" says p)[47].

---

43   2nd ed., vol. I, pp. 659-666.
44   Cf. ch. XII:
45   'The Philosophy of Logical Atomism', pp. 218-227.
46   Cf. J. Wisdom, *Logic & Constructions*, Volume XLIII, n169, 1934, pp.120–122, loc. cit p. 55n.
47   Cf. *Tractatus Logico-Philosophicus*, 5.54; 5.541;5.542; 5.5421; 5.5422. Cf. also J. Griffin, Op. *cit.*, p. 131; summarising the divergence between the two authors, Griffin notes that "The relation involved in a judgement is not between a person and the constituents of a fact, as Russell argues, but rather a relation between a psychical fact and the dense judgement. By saying that 'A judges p' one does not assert that A as a person stands in some relation to a fact. What is asserted is that in A's mind there is a psychical fact that has certain properties, the properties that any fact that depicts p must have".

The analysis of intensional constructs remained, however, one of the most tenacious knots of the extensional interpretation of language, which contributed to the rejection of reductionist analysis and to the so-called "revolt against logical atomism".[48] All the major philosophical analysts attempted to provide alternative interpretations to Russell's without, however, succeeding in effectively refuting the thesis to which he had reluctantly led his analysis.[49] The desire to uphold the theory of the extensionality of language and the related theory of truth as correspondence, the antecedents of which are to be found in the doctrine of external relations, in that of descriptions and classes as logical constructions, led Russell to an atomism that Urmson describes as "liberal and heterodox",[50] especially when compared to the views of the early Wittgenstein, and that would prepare the way for the overcoming of this theory. This heterodoxy is expressed, as we have seen, above all in the recognition of other irreducible facts besides the atomic ones. Alongside the facts corresponding to the intentional constructs examined above, Russell introduced also *negative facts*. These facts were not, however, recognised alongside the particular and general facts, but were based on another distinction, that of positive and negative, which was meant to safeguard the principle of truth as correspondence that seemed compromised unless it was admitted that the falsity of a proposition such as "Socrates is alive" derives from its lack of correspondence with a fact, i.e. the fact corresponding to the proposition "Socrates is not alive".[51] Again, the undermining of the general theory of atomism that such an acknowledgement entailed

---

48 Cf. G. Bergmann, 'The Revolt Against the Logical Atomism', The Philosophical Quarterly (1950-), vol. 7, n. 29), pp. 323-339 repr. in Meaning and Existence (Madison: univ. of Wisconsin Press, 1960.

49 See R. Carnap, *Logical Syntax of Language,* paragraphs 67 and 69 and *Meaning and Necessity,* Chicago, 1947, par. *32; Willard.* V. O., Quine, *From a Logical Point of View,* ch. VIII; I. C. Lewis, *An Analysis of Knowledge and Valuation,* La Salle, 1946, pp. 39, 41; F. P. Ramsey, *Facts and Propositions.*

50 *Philosophical Analysis.,* p. 190 ff.

51 "The Philosophy of Logical Atomism", pp. 211-215.

led other philosophers, among them Wisdom,[52] and Ramsey[53] to try to provide alternative analyses of undoubted interest but which failed to refute, on the argumentative ground proposed by Russell, his theses.

The third type of facts, irreducible to atomic facts, recognised by Russell, are the general facts that form the subject of the fifth lecture on atomism. At first, the orthodox atomist thesis will be adopted, according to which knowledge of all atomic facts should give us an "inventory of the world". According to this thesis, general propositions such as "All A's are B" and existential propositions such as "There are men" could be analysed in terms of enumeration and true-functional disjunction, respectively; but Russell considered this analysis erroneous because the general proposition "All men are mortal" does not merely enumerate a set of particular facts. It adds to the enumeration the further notion that the particular facts considered are 'all'. The general proposition is therefore not part of the true-functional analysis because it makes an assertion about an open class, i.e. composed of an "indefinite" number of particular facts that, being indefinite, cannot be enumerated. This consideration led him to consider the knowledge of general propositions as primitive and to admit the existence of general facts,[54] irreducible to atomic facts.

For the purposes of a deeper understanding of the intertwining of the different elements of Russell's philosophy, it is useful to note that as early as 1914 he had argued this thesis on the epistemological level. He had in fact stated that experience gives us knowledge of particulars but 'we seem to have as well knowledge of general propositions which we do not learn from experience and which are not inferable from experience'. The sum of particulars does not in fact logically imply general propositions; 'there is therefore a general knowledge that does not derive from sense, and part of this knowledge is not attained by deduction but is original'.[55]

---

52   *Logical Constructions,* quoted in *Mind,* 1931, p. 188-216
53   "Facts and Propositions", p. 163, ff.
54   Cf. "The Philosophy of Logical Atomism", p. 235.
55   Cf. *Our Knowledge of the External World,* p. 66, The critique of induction
     configured in this argumentation would later be taken up and developed

Russell had no followers in these theses of his; on the contrary, the other analytic philosophers, first among them Wittgenstein[56], tried to provide alternative conceptions in an attempt to stem the erosion of the foundations of atomism represented by the Russellian heterodoxy consisting of the multiplication of irreducible facts.

Contributions to the elucidation of this complex problem were again numerous, but often the sharpness of the analyses did not lead to philosophically remunerative convincing results, so that sometimes the authors themselves later rejected their own arguments in support of a rigorous atomism, as is the case of Frank Ramsey [57] and Ludwig Wittgenstein[58] himself- Alongside these two, another of the most relevant contributions was that made by John Wisdom in *Logical Constructions*[59].

It is no coincidental that our examination concludes with an indication of the special facts admitted by Russell in his atomism.

---

in another context by Karl Popper, becoming one of the main nuclei of epistemology, especially British epistemology. Cf. K. R. Popper *The Logic of Scientific Discovery,*

56 Prior to the *Tractatus,* Wittgenstein had shown his dissent from Russell's theory in *Notes On Logic* of 1913. Cf. L. Wittgenstein, *Notebooks* 1914-16, Oxford, 1961.

57 In the essay "Facts and Propositions" of 1927, cit., p. 169, he supported the thesis of the *Tractatus,* while in a later essay of 1929 entitled "General Propositions and Causality", in *The Foundations of Mathematics,* he stated that, since general propositions, although appearing to be such, are not conjunctions of atomic ones, they cannot be considered authentic propositions at all, and he interpreted them as general rules from which one can derive partial propositions tending to regulate the behaviour of individuals in specific circumstances.

58 The most complete version of his conception of the generality in a true-functional sense is found in *Tractatus,* 5.52, 5.5262, A review of this viewpoint can be found in the *Philosophische Bemerkungen,* Oxford 1964, IX, pp. 115 ff.

59 This essay offers a complete analysis whose central thesis is, in very simplified terms, that while general propositions cannot be analysed as enumerations or disjunctions of atomic facts, they do not assert a new type of irreducible fact. It is always the atomic facts that verify or falsify them. Their peculiarity consists in a defect of depicted capacity whereby they comprehensively state all atomic facts without explicitly asserting them individually.

We intend by this to emphasise the dual function exercised by this philosopher in English analytical philosophy. In addition to being the initiator of logical atomism, he was its most acute internal critic, enabling it to be overcome. When we referred to Russell's infanticide at the beginning of this chapter by quoting one of his expressions, we meant to emphasise the remarkable skill and courage that he had to overcome his own ideas that appeared to him, on closer examination, erroneous or unsatisfactory. It was precisely this critique that first brought out, albeit indirectly, the impossibility of reductive analysis and led the second and third generation of philosophical analysts to adopt, inspired above all by Wittgenstein, the two slogans: "don't ask for meaning, ask for use" and "every assertion has its logic", thus paving the way for descriptive analysis.

CHAPTER FIVE
THE PROBLEM OF METHOD

Philosophy as a kind of science

The functional link between methodological discourse and metaphysics would seem, *prima facie,* very tenuous in analytical philosophies. Nothing appears more free from metaphysical implications than an investigation grounded more on the neutral decomposition of reality than its interpretation in speculative terms. But although this functional link does not appear conspicuous, it is, nonetheless only less superficial, not less solid, even where the proponents of analytical and reductive philosophies seem only partly aware of it.[1]

The development of analytical philosophy in the broadest sense, i.e. all those systems of thought that reject the speculative method of enquiry and attribute a central place to the logical analysis of language is closely linked from one side to the research of Frege and Meinong and to those of Moore and Russell on the other. Russell's contribution to contemporary thought, focused here, has been vast and profound, and it can be said that there is no philosophical enquiry that he has not tackled or problematised.

Although vast and manifold, Russell's contribution has been above all logical and methodological, and this leads to a number of considerations. On the one hand, the functional character of the methodological approach implies, in general that an examination of the method is ultimately resolved in an evaluation of the conceptual and doctrinal content of philosophy in general and of Russell's philosophy in particular. Secondly, and consequently, the

---

1   See J. A. Feibleman, *Inside the Great Mirror,* pp. 13-14.

examination of the method cannot and must not exhaust itself in the investigation, albeit careful and detailed, of its technicalities (which are also of considerable importance), but needs to go further as far as the discovery of its metaphysical presuppositions, in a framework in which the distinction of form and content does not remain isolated but contribute to a unitary interpretative analysis.

Even before Adorno's deep analyses acquainted us with a typology in which emotional and sensual musical gluttons, devourers of isolated sound stimuli or undifferentiated ensembles, were contrasted with lucid and analytical listeners who, like the conductor, manage to grab the formal structure of the pieces,[2] the contrast between structural or vertical listening and emotional listening had been put forward by Russell in the context of a discourse on the correct method of philosophising. There he drew an analogy between the philosopher and the conductor, or rather between the analytical philosopher, conductor or expert listener on the one hand and the distracted or emotional listener and speculative philosopher on the other.

> A person without musical training, if he hears a symphony, acquires a vague general impression of the whole, whereas the conductor, as you may see from his gestures, is hearing a total which he minutely analyses into its several parts. The merit of analysis is that it gives knowledge not otherwise obtainable.[3]

Just as the conductor or the expert listener interpret and listen analytically to the musical text, summing up in the listening the succession of the various moments (past, present and future) in such a way that they make complete sense and are able to distinctly grasp even simultaneous complexities"[4], the 'philosopher correctly interprets and 'listens' to reality only if he adopts an analytical rather than speculative approach, if, that is to say, by applying a logical-analytical method of enquiry, he gives philosophical research a

---

2   Cf. Th.W.Adorno, *Einleitung in die Musiksoziologie* (Frankfurt, Surkkamp, 1962), p. 7-13.
3   B. Russell, *My Philosophical Development,* p. 169.
4   Cf. Ch. W. Adorno, cit., p. 7.

scientific configuration in the sense that he identifies as philosophy a well-defined field of enquiry and a rigorous methodology not anchored exclusively to the more or less brilliant personality of the thinker.

Such a philosophy, or rather such a methodology of philosophical enquiry, was never really meant as a reversal or a distortion of the traditional subject matter. On the contrary, in spite of his great contribution to the characterisation of contemporary thought, Russell remained in a certain sense a classical philosopher. An indirect proof of this may be given by the consideration of the analytical philosophy proper, developed at Oxford between the two wars (the analysis of language as an *practice* aimed at eliminating what may be misleading in linguistic expressions irrespective of a precise ontological focus or reference of language to facts). Although this philosophical practice springs from the analytical matrix of Russell and the early Wittgenstein, is experienced by its proponents as a rejection and a revolt against it Russellian atomism[5].

The breadth and depth of the subject matter is perhaps the most distinctive feature of Russell's philosophical contribution, but undoubtedly the attempt to determine the philosophical method is one of the most significant components of his research.

The great difficulties that his methodological approach has had to face lie, in our opinion, in the only supposed autonomy of the

---

5   Cf. J.O.Urmson, *The Philosophical Analysis,* pp.27-44 and 97-98. In this essay, Urmson examines the transition from an analysis based on the assumption of the structural isomorphism of language and reality as that proposed by Russell, to the so-called therapeutic analysis aimed not at knowledge of reality, but at "dispelling perplexities, avoiding misunderstandings and unmasking absurd theories". An analysis that stems from the 'second' Wittgenstein, theoretician of common language and whose major representatives are Wisdom, Ryle, Waismann and Austin. In his *My Philosophical Development,* p.161, Russell polemically pointed out his position with respect to the analysts of the second generation as follows. "In common with all philosophers before W II, my fundamental aim has been to understand the world as well as may be and to separate what may count as knowledge from what must be rejected as unfounded opinion .... But we are now told instead that it is not 'the world we are to try to understand but only sentences...',

sphere of the methodological, in its very nature of a pseudo-problem. This problematic is in fact articulated in two closely connected but conceptually distinct moments. On the one hand, the determination of the nature, the 'depth' of philosophy, i.e. its theoretical content, its object and, on the other, the determination of its status in relation to other forms of human thought and, in particular, its place with respect to science or, as is sometimes said with an obvious petition of principle, to *other* sciences.

Although Russell's contribution to methodological discourse has in some sense largely determined subsequent developments in philosophical research, it is difficult to share entirely the opinion of some scholars according to which Russell did leave 'illuminating' descriptions of his method of enquiry[6]. As is sometimes the case in the writings of this philosopher, who has also been a fine scholar and a great narrator,[7] clarity and verbal lucidity conceal sometimes obscurity of substantial conceptual ambiguity. It would seem, therefore, that the explicit methodological declarations, which are rather meagre and for the most part very general, lend themselves to many conflicting interpretations, and rather than relying on them, the interpreter should preferably travel backwards to reconstruct his method from an examination of its applications.[8] It should also be stressed that the logical-analytical method is so rooted in and functional to the metaphysical presuppositions of his thought that any attempt at an isolated thematization aimed as Russell proposed, to be expressed "in precise maxims"[9] runs the risk of leading to an inadequate interpretation of his thought, an interpretation that escapes

---

6   See E. Ramsden-Eames, *Bertrand Russell's Theorv of Knowledge,* p. 58.
7   It is barely to be remembered that Russell in 1950 was also the winner of the Nobel prize for Literature "in recognition of his varied and significant writings in which he defended humanitarian ideals and freedom of thought".
8   My opinion is that the optimism of Ramsden Eames is generally due to the interpretation in methodological terms of features of Russell's philosophy that sometimes seem to be metaphysical and ontological presuppositions acting covertly although not clearly spelled out
9   Cf. B. Russell, *Our Knowledge of the External World,* p.7; *Mysticism and Logic,* p.209.

the intimate bond that in his thought, as almost in all philosophies, links methodology and theory, methodology and *Weltanschauung*.

The substance of Russell's discourse on method (the affinity with Descartes is anything but superficial) can be briefly summarised as follows: philosophy, unlike the positive or 'hard' sciences, has made no progress. Indeed one of its characteristics is the continual questioning of all its assumptions and even its object. By contrast, gradual and steady progress has been made in the positive sciences, the knowledge of which has a profoundly different formal and logical structure. In order for real progress to be possible, it is therefore necessary for philosophy to learn from science and to aim at a type of knowledge that resembles the structure of scientific knowledge in the way it is constituted and grows, even if not in its content, which is its own.

The achievement of such a goal – the structural "scientificization" of philosophical knowledge – demands, however, in his view, a reform of method, because it is precisely an inadequate methodology that has done philosophy such a poor service. The method of philosophy must be scientific in its general inspiration but is particularly characterised by the application of logic and analysis to specific problems.

A correct method of philosophical enquiry must therefore be scientific, and the methodological "scientificity" of philosophising lies in its logical-analytical character. The critical terms of this programme are quite explicit; the correct philosophical investigation must abandon the insecure path of speculation and metaphysics or at least a certain metaphysics and the search for global solutions that are either completely true or completely false and have so far all been shown to be completely false.

The main matrix of this mistake in its perspective is, according to Russell, the epistemological anthropocentrism that led man to refer reality to himself by interpreting it in multiple but similar ways on the level of subjectivism. Russell has instead always maintained that human experience represents only a tiny and secondary part of the universe.

One must first ask what is the nature of "scientificity", and what Russell means by the word scientific. And so again, what does it mean when he says that the method is logical-analytical. The meaning of these terms is far from unambiguous; indeed, they are overloaded with layers of meanings historically overlapping one another. They cannot therefore be considered abstractly methodological, i.e. metaphysically neutral, because they actually conceal deeper ontological implications and metaphysical presuppositions that need to be made explicit.

The components of Russell's methodology are therefore, in very broad terms, "scientificity", logic and analysis. We will now try to examine these determinations in some more detail.

The attempt to make philosophy a science is far from new in the history of thought. In the modern age, both Bacon's work with all its ambiguities and that of Descartes largely configure this aspiration; it is therefore not on the affirmation of pure principle that the originality of Russellian perspectives may rest. If we consider that the theoretical debate around the nature and general form of scientific knowledge is still far from being exhausted and constitutes the specific field of theoretical investigation of the philosophy of science, the claim that philosophy must not only be inspired by science but even "become a science" opens up a chasm of unresolved problems.

What does it mean that philosophy must be *inspired by science;* that it *it must be based* on science; that it must *become* a science?

The use of these three expressions[10] not only betrays the semantic equivocity but also suggests the conceptual misunderstanding underlying such analogies and equations. To be inspired is different from becoming and grounded on. The way science and philosophy relate to each other is in other words loaded with problems that are also reflected in the verbal expression of this relationship.

Russell seems to conceive the "scientificization" of philosophy in at least two ways, one corresponding to the expression "inspiring" and the second to "grounding" and *becoming.* We shall call the first mode generic and the second specific. Philosophy is scientific in a generic sense when it draws that inspiration, i.e. motives, from science rather than from religion or ethics. He takes somehow for

---

10   Cf. B. Russell, On Scientific Method in Philosophy *97-124* p. 127; *Our Knowledge of the External World,* p. 9,

granted that these are the sources of philosophical thought, and this is also psychologically reflected in the "three passions simple but overwhelmingly strong [that] have governed his life: the longing for love, the search for knowledge and unbearable pity for the suffering of mankind"[11] that, mediated as they seem by intellectualism, do not seem to be passions at all, and which in any case, due to their mutual and absolute isolation, seem to be inherent in different personalities. The "scientificity" we called generic is characterised, in short, as neutrality of investigation with respect to results and methods. Neutrality should guarantee, in a certain way, against arbitrary preconceptions or rejections of any results, based on value judgements or an anthropocentric apptoach. Just as the sciences have progressed since they ceased to commensurate the validity of investigations with the greater or lesser dignity of their object, so philosophy as well cannot progress as long as philosophical theories relating to the understanding of the world are influenced by human desires or considerations of good and evil that, according to Russell, should'nt have any place in the rational search for truth.[12]

Much of the classical philosophical systems and metaphysics are characterised, he argues, by the intrusion of ethical elements that are fundamentally foreign to the philosophical understanding of the world and are "not submitted to the facts, a submission that is the essence of the scientific temperament".[13]

From this attitude one should deduce the extraneousness of ethics to philosophical research in general and to Russell's in particular. On the contrary, it is well known that behind many of Russell's writings there often lurked a moralist or, at any rate, a keen observer of political and social facts. Russell's interest in these problems is, moreover, testified by many writings with political, social, ethical and educational content [14] even if the philosophical nature in the strict sense of these writings is perhaps a bit weak. Rather, they should be

---

11 Russell, B. *The Autobiography of Bertrand Russell*, vol. I, p. 1

12 Cf. *Our Knowledge of the External World*, p. 38.

13 Cf. *Mysticism* and *Logic*, cit., p. 140.

14 Cf. *Power a Social Analysis,*; *Roads to Freedom,*; *Principles of Social Reconstruction*; *The Practice and Theory of Bolshevism,* ibi; *On Education,* ibid; *Marriage and Morals*. Towards the end of his life he

framed within the particular thesis of the division of his fundamental interests mentioned earlier and their mutual independence.

Among the philosophers who were predominantly inspired by religion and ethics and thus somehow saw the world through the spectacles of ought-to-be, Russell counts Plato, Spinoza and Hegel, while Leibniz, Locke and Hume would be more 'scientific'; others such as Descartes, Berkeley and Kant would be influenced by both ethical and scientific stimuli.

Typical, according to Russell, of philosophies burdened with religious and ethical mortgages is the presence of concepts such as the *universe* or *good and evil,* all of which are fundamentally irrelevant for the philosophical problematic. The first because it configures an erroneous concept of generality. Even though the philosophy should consist of general statements, the kind of generality that underlies statements about the universe is an improper generality insofar as it is collective and therefore confused, whereas the correct generality of philosophical statements has a distributive[15] and not a collective character, in other words it concerns the world as a complex aggregate of components and not as a unity. The concepts of good and evil, as mentioned above, denounce the projection of ethical elements into philosophical enquiry, which Russell considered completely gratuitous and unjustified[16] on the basis of his rejection of any anthropocentrism.

---

    gave also life with Sartre to the Russell Tribunal for war crimes in Viet-Nam.

15   This criticism is linked more precisely to the propositional conception of knowledge and thus to the fundamental logical component of method. It will find significant development in the framework of the Russellian theory of the meaning and resolution of complex symbols.

16   For the purposes of a correct determination of Moore's enormous and decisive contribution to the elaboration of a new philosophical methodology that was to form the basis of later analytical developments in English thought, it is useful to note, with regard to ethical neutrality, that as early as 1903 Moore had already proposed the independence of the ethical sphere from the theoretical sphere with the famous argument of the 'naturalistic fallacy'. Cf. *Principia Ethica.* p.15. For a detailed use of Moore reconsideration of the use of the fallacy cf. also Ayer, p. 229.

Alongside this scientificity, which we called generic, and which should pertain in some way to the philosopher's general attitude, and to his outlook, namely to what Russell calls the scientific temperament, there is another, much more significant one, on which the fruitfulness and originality of Russell's philosophy substantially rests. This second aspect of scientificity, or rather its more specific developments, will characterise the logical and analytical inspiration of his philosophy.

A first determination of the scientific character of philosophy both methodologically and in terms of content lies in its autonomy.

> Philosophy – says Russell – is not a shortcut to the same kind of results as those of the other sciences; if it is to be a genuine study, it must have a province of its own and aim at results that the other sciences can neither prove or disprove.[17]

This is a very significant statement. Above all, it claims an autonomy of research field and in this sense demands a place and status for philosophy alongside the other sciences. This implies that the philosopher is a scientist among others and that reciprocal relations are horizontal relations, so to speak, and not hierarchical. The last observation reveals, however, a kind of breakdown in this peer to peer relationship. Indeed, the modern scientific landscape does not seem to be characterised by this normative atomism. The wide margin of interdisciplinarity that characterises the different sciences means that the results of a given discipline are often refuted or confirmed by those of another, so that there seems to be a contradiction between the intention to demystify the crowning role and general synthesis that philosophy has played in the tradition and this unwillingness to engage in the thematic confrontations that the equal status of the sciences would demand and that practice testifies to.

In this context, the stress on the eminently methodological rather than content-based character of the scientific vocation of philosophy is particularly important.

---

17   B. Russell, *Our Knowledge of the External World, p.* 27.

"Much philosophy inspired by science has gone astray through preoccupation with the *results* momentarily supposed to have been achieved. It is not results, but *methods* that can be transferred with profit from the sphere of special sciences to the sphere of philosophy".[18]

It is, in short, a rather problematic parity, a parity similar to King Arthur's relation to the other round table knights, that is to say, rather clumsy. Among equals it is not possible for anyone to be more equal. Russell's attitude in this regard has never been fully clarified. The scientific bias here clashes with the philosopher's own radical problemacity. The relation between science and philosophy seems a dead-end street, a problem that by definition seems to be impossible to solve either by appealing to philosophy or by appealing to science. Russell was perhaps aiming at a philosophy as rigorous as physics but capable of retaining a radical problematicity that would allow it to transcend pure scientific character by incorporating it into a higher level, perhaps that very same level of the political or social that he had wanted to oust or at least isolate from the sphere of scientific philosophy.

What shapes to a greater extent than any other the character of specific scientificity of Russell's method of investigation is the intention to arrive at the determination of a way of proceeding susceptible of being expressed in maxims and in general principles;[19] capable, that is, of becoming, to an ever greater extent, autonomous or at least less and less dependent on the personality of the researcher and, consequently, such as to profoundly affect the individualistic character of philosophical research. It is also true, however, that Russell does not underestimate the importance of individual skill and insight in philosophical research:

> When everything has been done that can be done by method, a stage
> is reached where only direct philosophic vision can carry matter further.
> Here only genius will avail [...] As a rule, is some new effort of logical
> imagination some glimpse of a possibility, never conceived before, and

---

18   B. Russell, 'On Scientific Method' in p.98.
19   Cf. B.Russell, *Our Knowledge of the External World*, p. 7.

then the direct perception that this possibility is realised in the case in question.[20] (*ibid.*, p. 245)

It is in this framework that the concept of "progress" applied to philosophical research takes on importance; a progress that can be assimilated to that introduced by Galileo in physics[21], i.e. a progress that accumulates step by step, "piece by piece". It is clear now why, according to Russell, philosophy inspired by the scientific method must necessarily have an analytical structure. It will have to break down complex problems into more numerous but simpler ones; and, above all, it will have to seek partial results so that when a system turns out to be wrong, it will be only partially and not totally wrong and each philosopher may start all over again, being able to use even if only partially the results of his predecessors.[22] Such a programme unequivocally shows the rejection, on the one hand, of the great metaphysical systems of the philosophical tradition – although in fact in Russell does act – and not entirely unconsciously – a solid metaphysical structure and a positive conception of philosophy as a factual lpractice engaged in the gradual decoding of the structure of reality.[23]

---

20 See also Popper's theses on scientific discovery in *The Logic of Scientific Discovery, p.???*.

21 cf. B. Russell, *Our Knowledge of the External World,* p. 246.

22 Cf. On Scientific Method in Philosophy' p.113 Here it is particularly evident how great is the lesson that Russell has drawn from Bacon and Descartes. "The second (rule) was to divide every problem taken to study into as many smaller parts as were possible and necessary to solve it better. The third, to conduct one's thoughts in order, beginning with the simplest and easiest objects to know, and ascending little by little, as if by degrees, to the knowledge of the most complex, and supposing an order even among those of which the one does not naturally precede the other". Descartes, *Discours de la Methode,* Subsequent research on history and philosophy of science, rejected the notion of progress based on the model of linear accumulation. Cf. C. Kuhn, *The structure of Scientific Revolutions,*

23 In outlining his philosophical perspective in the course of the eight lectures on logical atomism, Russell declared that he wanted to illustrate a certain logical theory and on the basis of this a certain metaphysics. In short a logical theory, underlied by a metaphysical substratum: i.e. a

Philosophy as Analysis

As we have seen, Russell advocates a new method that would guarantee philosophy a similar progress to that achieved by the other sciences. This method need to be inspired by science, not by the results but by the methods of science; he calls this his logical-analytical method. We have thus far examined the general aspects and meaning of philosophical scientificity, but this constitutes little more than an approach to understanding Russell's philosophy. Many more substantial difficulties in interpreting and evaluating his philosophy arise when we try to examine more precisely the sense and meaning of logic and analysis as he understands them. The sense of geometrical clarity that generally inspires a superficial reading of Russell's writings is destined to crumble as one delves deeper into its implications, where a much more intricate web appears; a set of correlations with the preceding philosophical tradition and a tangled web of methodological motifs with theoretical elements and with fungible but essentially unresolved assumptions, and above all that tangle of seemingly heterogeneous planes (epistemology, logic, metaphysics, analysis of language), which hardly lend themselves to a unified interpretation.

A great question is: in what sense is Russell's philosophy analytical and in what sense is this analysis logical if it transcends the merely logical plane to present itself as an interpretation of the extralinguistic structure and our ways of knowing it? The answer to this question may hardly be be univocal, especially because, as we shall see, while the elucidation of the concept of analysis does not appear particularly difficulty *prima facie*, the difficulties arise when we consider that Russell's conception of logic goes beyond the traditional distinctions of deductive and inductive logic to assume a productive character, so to speak, in the sense that it produces

---

metaphysic grounded by the presupposition of isomorphism between the logical structure of language and the logical structure of extralinguistic reality. The many difficulties of such an assumption have been highlighted by Urmson and Max Black, among others. See respectively, Urmson, J. O. *The Philosophical Analysis*, pp. 27-41 and 'Russell Philosophy of Language', p. 254..

hypotheses and that analyticity is an intrinsic feature of what Russell means by logic.

The separate treatment of the analytical and the logical components therefore have all the limitations inherent in interpretive devices that, while constituting a phase in the penetration of a thought, necessarily postulate their overcoming.

Russell's method is analytical insofar as it accepts and makes its own the Cartesian maxim of breaking down complex problems into simple ones and in its conception of gradualness and philosophical progress. This however leaves open two major problems, one of a normative nature and the other more specifically metaphysical, which can be formulated as follows: on what basis does the legitimacy of analysis rest? What is the nature of *the analysandum?* The answer to these questions, in addition to configuring and involving Russell's entire gnoseological and metaphysical perspective, reflects the confrontation that opposed Bradley's monistic idealism to the prospect of a pluralist realism and atomism underlying Russell's *Weltanschauung*. That his is a *weltanschauung* and not a new metaphysically neutral method appears clearly for at least two reasons. On the one hand, the program of a decomposition as such, although not new in the history of thought, does not offer a self-foundation, acting as a legitimation. It is opposed not to another method but to the global solutions peculiar in metaphysics and speculative philosophies. In the guise of a methodology, it conceals the presupposition – which in Russell's philosophy will ultimately always remain unjustified – of the legitimacy of decomposition and analysis. This presupposition, on the other hand, is in turn rooted in two fundamental axioms that are metaphysical and not methodological. The notion that the reality is made up of a multitude of variously aggregating but mutually independent elements is what Russell at later stages of his analysis would call *particulars*. this assumption is what substantiates the pluralist view of the real. This plurality of objects and its aggregative structure – this is the second axiom – is depicted in the structure of logic of propositions. "I will assume that there is an objective complexity of the world and that it is mirrored by the complexity of propositions".[24] In short, we have here a fundamental structural isomorphism that legitimises the investigation of language as a means of discovering the structure of extralinguistic reality. And it is also on this assumption that the *propositional character* of knowledge characterises Russellian philosophy and his conception according to which logic is the "essence of philosophy".

Such a perspective – namely his logical atomism – is, as we saw in the previous chapter, fraught with difficulties; first and foremost, that of the equivocal entanglement in which the method of investigation and its underlying *Weltanschauung* are entangled. Russell, on the other hand, showed in more than one occasion that he was aware of these difficulties. At the time he wrote *The Principles of Mathematics,* he was not entirely convinced of the legitimacy of the method of analysis.[25] Indeed, the entire English idealist school maintained that analysis is falsification, the mutilation of reality. In short, the justification of analysis is closely linked not as much to methodological considerations but to a metaphysical perspective or rather to a world view that, as such, is barely susceptible to justification.

In 1924, in a paper on logical atomism in which he expounds the general framework of his ideas on the relation between language and reality in a kind of manifesto and in a more popular form, Russell basically confirms his inability to adequately ground his fundamental theoretical choices.

> There is nothing – he states – in logic that can help one choose between monism and pluralism or between the theses that there are ultimate relational facts and the theses that there are not. I have made my choice in favour of pluralism and relations on empirical grounds, after having convinced myself that the arguments put forward in support of the opposing theses are not valid.[26]

---

24   The Philosophy of Logical Atomism in *Logic and Knowledge,* p. 197
25   Cf. *The Principles of Mathematics,* p. 241-2; 466-7.
26   Logical Atomism in *Logic and Knowledge,* p. 338-9.

If we consider that logic for Russell is not traditional logic but expands to the point of coinciding in its modalities and scope with philosophical research, the assertion sounds like a surrender and a serious downsizing of philosophy's ability to provide fundamental answers, even if this is, on the other hand, perfectly consistent with the thesis of the scientificisation of philosophy, and the parcellarity and gradualness of its results gained "piece by piece". Monism and pluralism are therefore not terms of an incontrovertible determination but different opportunities for choice, a choice made on those empirical foundations that if they are to be foundations and not *Weltanschauungen* require precisely that they be founded. These intrinsic limitations of Russell's thought will emerge with greater clarity, as we have seen, in his doctrine of logical atomism.

The Propositional character of Knowledge

The study of logic had an important functional character in Russell with respect to the solution of the gnoseological problem and with respect to his metaphysics. Russell's logic, taken in the broad sense is neither deductive nor inductive. Although it includes both, it transcends the two traditional determinations [27]and identifies itself plainly with philosophy.

> Every philosophical problem, says Russell, when subjected to the necessary analysis and purification process, either turns out not to be truly philosophical at all or turns out to be logical in the sense in which we use the word.[28]

Let us take a closer look at the reasons why for him every philosophical problem is actually a logical one and what Russell does mean by logical; what is the scope of logic, its scientific status; what are its objects and the limits of logical enquiry. It is necessary to bear in mind that he inherited from Bacon and Descartes, and made his own, the absorption of the logical problem within the

---

27   Cf. Margaret MacDonald, *Russell and MacTaggart* p. 322-335.
28   *Our Knowledge of the external world,* p. 42.

gnoseological one. This entailed, on the one hand, the rejection of the abstract character of logic as it was traditionally understood and, on the other hand, although the two are closely connected, the end of an autonomous logic independent from the other fields of philosophical reflection.

In several places Russell calls upon the logician to maintain a robust "sense of reality"[29] and it would be this sense of reality that would drive him in 1905 to reject Meinong's theory of meaning, overcoming even the positions expressed in the *Principles* regarding existence, in order to adopt a new theory of meaning. The one underlying his theory of descriptions. But before examining this new logic, we need to consider also another component that is prejudicial and that grounds the basis on which the conception of logic as the essence of philosophy rests: i.e. the relation between language and knowledge. The fundamental character of knowledge is for him that of being *propositional.* We know the world through judgements that are configured into propositions that assert or deny facts. Since logic studies the elements of propositions and their structures and establishes the legitimacy of some types of structures and the illegitimacy of others in relation to truth and falsehood (seen by Russell, as a characteristic of propositions in their relation to empirical data) logic is the cognitive instrument *par excellence,* even if not the *prius* epistemological. The belief in the propositional character of knowledge opens up serious interpretative problems, some of which are first of all, historical, pertinent to the exact place of Russell's philosophy in the empiricist tradition; others are related to a more precise determination of the traits of this philosophical perspective that will constitute a true turning point. However, this centrality of logic does not have the power of self-grounding and rests on metaphysical assumptions.

The propositional character of knowledge is thus the feature of his philosophy that more than any other distinguishes his empiricism

---

29   "Logic," he argued in his *Introduction to Mathematical Philosophy,* "must not admit unicorns any more than zoology; in fact, logic deals with the real world in the same way as zoology, albeit in more abstract and broad terms.

from classical empiricism in general and Humean empiricism in particular. This reveals a trait that, at one and the same time, constitutes the originality of Russell's thought, linking it, however, as we have seen, to a philosophical tradition – the idealist one – that is far removed from his perspective.

Russell, however, is also Hume's most faithful heir, but whereas Hume understands the theory of knowledge as a research that takes place on a plane of psychological analysis, i.e. the plane of the actual and factual succession of representations of the empirical self, Russell frees theory of knowledge from this limitation and, accepting both the idealist lesson and Frege's teachings, sets up a theory of knowledge that overcomes the traditional antilogical bias of empiricism.

From a certain point of view Russell's theory of knowledge is fundamentally Humean. In both philosophers the central role, the *prius* epistemological, is constituted by the sense data that underpin all our knowing. The similarity goes so far that the skeptical conclusion of Humean empiricism – that fails to overcome the prison of impressions and ideas – finds a counterpart and rather an analogue in Russellian constructivist gnoseology when, in an attempt to avoid undue inferences, it tries to dispense with postulating the existence of the self and the external world and *constructs* all knowledge of common sense and of physics from the only certain elements: sensory data. There are, however, significant differences, and one in particular is such that makes the two empiricists' thinking somehow incommensurable.

According to Hume, all our knowledge comes from experience, which consists of perceptions that Hume distinguishes into impressions and ideas. However, it does not only originate from experience, but is exhausted with it. It is above all on the declared impossibility of rationally overcoming the *internal spectacle* that the sceptical conclusion of Hume's empiricism fundamentally rests.

His theory of knowledge has the structure of a psychological atomism with all the difficulties that such a position entails. In order to have knowledge it is not enough the acquisition of individual impressions and ideas; these need to be united according to organic principles on the basis of a structure. The individual impressions must join on the basis of rules, and this union requires a structure, i.e. a grammar and syntax of thought, i.e. a logical fabric. Humean analysis does not put forward a general theory of thought but only an analysis of its components. It is as if the individual parts of a machine were listed and described, but the assembly diagram and mutual connections were not given. In this way, it is not easy to understand how the machine works. In short, the individual parts – like the representative content of impressions and ideas – contain no indication of their place in the machine. The representative content of impressions and ideas is in itself insufficient, for example, to guarantee the temporal reference.[30] Thus, in an analysis such as Hume's lacking a general theory of the articulation of thought, it is difficult to understand how an idea-remembrance of, say, a horse is distinguishable from an idea-expectation of a horse.

Differences between perceptions are differences in their representational content and thus any difference between ideas is an inadequate difference to determine the peculiar character that distinguishes, for example, a belief from an expectation. The concept of greater vividness that Hume often resorts to in order to explain such differences does not shed any more light because it is, so to speak, a kind of *deus ex machina,* an expedient that does not fit into the general theory, just as the mechanisms of the association of ideas are not theoretically justified.

Humean theory of knowledge therefore, caught between the two poles of atomism of representations and the psychologistic limits of gnoseological analysis, necessarily ran up against the stumbling block of the absence of a general theory of atomism of representations and the psychologistic limits of ideas. Russell has the merit of overcoming this difficulty. By breaking the traditional anti-logical bias of the empiricists, which confined theory of knowledge within the limits of a difficult associationism, he enabled it to be overcome.

The progress, on which much of British realist thought in some ways rests, is due on the one hand by the insertion of a propositional perspective into the pluralist atomism that characterises classical

---

30   See D.F.Pears, *Bertrand Russell and the British Tradition in Philosophy,* London 1967, pp. 29-31.

empiricism and, on the other, by the overcoming of its psychologist bias. This important step, loaded with consequences, will be mediated on both the methodological and theoretical levels by the practice of the analysis of language as an analysis of the ways of expressing the thought and thus of the central and primarily philosophical role of logic.

Nonetheless the overcoming of a psychologistic conception of the theory of knowledge does not end with Russell's original contribution. On the contrary, he inherited and shared the separation of philosophy and logic from psychology, advocated by the idealists' in general and Bradley above all. And yet the statement that the analysis of knowledge must start from the judgement or proposition and not from the idea or concept is to be considered a corner stone in Russell's philosophy. So becomes clear why, for him, logic is to be considered the 'essence of philosophy'. Logic, in short, acquires its philosophical value to the extent that it accesses a propositional conception of knowledge, which places the theory of judgement at the centre of investigation. The activity of the 'philosopher is therefore the reformulation of the propositions in which traditional philosophical problems are expressed, on the basis of the principles of legitimacy that are provided by logic. These principles tend to establish on a preliminary basis whether the problems are correctly posed, i.e. whether, when formulated in this way, they make sense and can be solved, or whether, on the other hand, a correct reformulation shows that the problems as they had been formulated do not exist and instead other problems arise or are even beyond human possibilities.[31]

---

31   It is in this sense that MacDonald states that Russell's analytical logical method can be considered neither deductive nor inductive but a way of elucidating the meaning of expression. Cf. *'Russell and McTaggart'* in Philosophy, p. 323. And it is also in this sense that M. calls it "a form of real and contextual definition". Cf. *Analysis and* Weitz *the Unity of Russell's Philosophy* p. 57. On the other hand, one cannot entirely agree with MacDonald's thesis when she seems to attribute to Russell a conception of language devoid or lacking metaphysical implications, a conception that rather configures the alleged neutrality of Oxonian analysts and not of Russell who not only affirmed the self-evident goal set

This philosophical project is implemented, as we have shown, through the mediation of logic. And here we have perhaps the most remarkable, and certainly the most fruitful and lasting contribution of Russell's thought: the reform of logic. However the logical conversion of philosophy and the liberation of the theory of knowledge from its psychologistic mortgage is also fundamentally a contribution of the English idealist school mediated by Bradley's critique of the empiricist concept of the idea. Nonetheless the degree of development to which, Russell and Whitehead led logic by extending its methods from the mathematical to philosophical research is perhaps the most brilliant contribution of Russell's genius. The intuition of the philosophical scope of logic is thus the *quid novi* that largely characterises his thought.

Russell distinguishes two areas of logic, one of which is certainly more congruent with the philosophical problem. The first area is that general and abstract theory consisting of general propositions devoid of any empirical reference. It basically asserts the truth of propositions of certain forms, based on absolutely formal connections. This logic thus constitutes a formal, deductive system. It is a rigorous but not empirical science. The propositions of pure mathematics fall, according to the thesis of the *Principia,* into this branch or sector of logic.

This deductive logic is analogous even if it can not be identified with classical logic. It is not identified with that because in the Russellian reform even of this first philosophical field it is not totally inscribed in the Aristotelian syllogistic structure, above all because predication does not exhaust its fundamental forms. Alongside the subject-predicate statements Russell recognises, as we have seen, those of relation that are not reducible to the first.[32] Such logic is however made up of precepts that "serve rather to explain to others

---

by his philosophy but also polemised with Oxonians who were inspired by the second Wittgenstein. Cf. *My Philosophical Development,* p. 161.

32   It is precisely on the irreducibility of relational forms that Russell rests one of the strongest arguments for pluralism. Cf. *The Principles of Mathematics,* cit., pp. 209-226.

– as Descartes said – things that are already known […]instead of learning them"[33]

Although there is an albeit instrumental relationship that links this logic to philosophical problematics in the sense that it helps to simplify through the use of symbolism if not the problems, the way of dealing with them, the logic that Russell considers the "essence of philosophy" is not this. It is not deductive but analytical and does not coincide at all with the traditional meaning. This second part investigates 'what propositions are and what forms they can have and enumerates the different kinds of general propositions'.[34]

It is very important to note, especially for the purpose of discussing the metaphysical implications of Russell's logic, that in another essay[35] Russell points out that this new logic enumerates not only propositions but also types of facts and the classification of the components of facts. It is precisely the search for the components of facts that configures the metaphysical character of Russellian logic.

There are two most unique features of the new logic: its analytical structure and its objects.

> The function of logic in philosophy as I shall try to show at a later stage is all important;, but I do not think its function is that which it has the classical tradition. In that tradition, logic becomes constructive through negation. Where a number of alternatives seem at first sight to be equally possible, logic is made to condemn all of them except one, and that one is then pronounced to be realised in the actual world. Thus the world is constructed by means of logic, with little or no appeal to concrete experience. The true function of logic is, in my opinion, exactly the opposite of this. As applied to matters of experience, it is analytic than constructive; taken *a priori* it shows the possibility of hitherto unsuspected alternatives, more often than the impossibility of alternatives which seemed *prima facie* possible.[36]

The critical reference to the classical tradition does not target Aristotle or scholastic logic but is an indirect attack to the monist

---

33 Descartes, René, *Discours de la Méthode* (Paris: Foucher, s.d.), p. 59
34 Cf. *Our Knowledge of the External World,* p. 18.
35 On the Scientific Method in Philosophy in *Mysticism and Logic*, p. 97.
36 *Our Knowledge of the External World,* p.18.

idealism advocated by Bradley and its condemnation of the world of experience relegated precisely on the basis of a judgement of contradiction to the limbo of appearances.

But the most interesting and innovative aspect of Russell's logic is its openness to experience. It is in this sense that logical analysis provides an inventory, not just of abstract possibilities, but of the structure of reality and thus transcends the domain of form. The new logic thus tends to identify itself with philosophical enquiry. Certainly this logic, which can indifferently be applied to the objects of experience or taken a priori, aroused some perplexity, and on this point one could legitimately question the judgement of a system-builder Russell.[37] The perplexity is even destined to increase if one considers that more or less at the same time Russell also argued that philosophical statements must be a priori and in any case such that they can neither be demonstrated nor refuted by empirical proofs. The difficulties of interpretation become almost arduous here. Logic for Russell is not an autonomous province of knowledge but only makes sense if it is taken in the context of the theory of knowledge. Now, although our knowledge arises from experience, it is not exhausted in it because the system of coordinating empirical data is not itself given and also because science also consists of general propositions that are not obtained as the sum of particular propositions. This knowledge is not empirical, it must be found in logic.

The attempt to weld these two levels, an empiricist theory of knowledge based on sense data and the need for rigour represented by the formal sciences, was probably the qualifying philosophical core of Russell's thought. This attempt failed. Nor have his successors succeeded in this task, who rather than solving unsolved problems, as often happens in philosophy, did overcome them by abandoning them; that is, by denying them as problems and identifying new ones.

---

37   Cf. C.D.Broad, "Critical and Speculative Philosophy" in *Contemporary English Philosophers,* edited by J. H. Muirhead (London: Allen & Unwin, 1924) pp 17-99. loc cit p. 19 for a discussion on this topic see also Nielsen, Kai 'Broad's Conception of Critical and Speculative Philosophy, Dialectica, Vol. 48, No. 1 (1994), pp. 47-64

SELECTED BIBLIOGRAPHY

Ayer, Alfred. J., 'Verification and Experience' *Proceedings of the Aristotelian Society,* vol. 37 (1936-37); reprinted in A.J. Ayer, (ed.) *Logical Positivism* (New York: Free Press 1959).

Ayer, A. J., *Russell and Moore: the Analytical Heritage* (London: Mac Millan, 1971).

Ayer, A. J., *Russell* (London: Collins, 1972).

Beattie, James, *Essays on the Nature and Immutability of Truth in Opposition to Sophistry and Skepticism; on Poetry and Music as they Affect the Mimi;- on Laughter and Ludicrous Compositions; on the Utility of Classical Learning,* (Edinburgh: Denham & Dick, 1776).

Bech, L.W., 'Constructions and Inferred Entities' in Brodbeck, M. & Feigl, H., Eds *Readings in the Philosophy of Science* (New York: Appleton Century Crofts, 1953).

Bell, D., *Bertrand Russell* (London: Betterworth,1972).

Bergmann, G. The Philosophical Quarterly (1950), vol. 7, n. 29 (ottobre 1957), pp. 323-339

Benjamin, A. C., 'The Logical Atomism of Bertrand Russell' (doctoral thesis), University of Michigan (1927).

Bergmann, G., 'The Revolt against Logical Atomism' in Klemke, E. D. (ed.) *Essays on Bertrand* Russell (Urbana: University of Illinois Press, 1970).

G.Bergmann, 'Russell on Particulars', *The Philosophical Review,* 56, (1947) pp. 59-72 reprinted in Klemke, (pp. 15-27)

Black, M., 'Russell's Philosophy of Language' in Schilpp, P. A. *The Philosophy of Bertrand Russell* (LaSalle: Open court, 1944, 4th ed 1971).

Bonfantini, M., 'La nozione di verità in Russell' *Aut Aut,* vol. 20, (1970).

Bradley, F. H., *Essays on Truth and Reality* (Oxford: Oxford University Press,1914).

Bradley, F. H. *The Principles of Logic 2 voll.* (Oxford: Oxford University Press,1883, 2nd ed. 1922).

Bradley, F. H., *Ethical Studies* (Oxford: Clarendon Press, 1927 (2nd). 1962).

Bradley, F. H., *Collected Essays* (Oxford: Oxford University Press, 1969).

Bradley, F. H., *Appearance and Reality* (London: Swan Sonnenschein, 1906).

Brentano, F. *Psychologie Vom Empirichen Standpunkt,* (Leipzig: Duncker & Humblot, 1874).

Broad, C. D., 'Critical and Speculative Philosophy' in J. H. Muirhead (ed.) *Contemporary English Philosophers* (London: Routledge, 1939).

Britton, C., 'Truth and Knowledge: Some Comments on Russell' *Analysis,* vol. 8 (1947-48).

Burns-Delisle, C., 'Note on Ockam's Razor' *Mind,* vol. 24, (1915).

Burns-Delisle, C., 'William of Ockam on Continuity' *Mind,* vol. 25, (1916).

Butcharov, P., 'On an Alleged Mistake of Logical Atomism' *Analysis,* vol. 19, (1958-59).

Butler, R. J., 'The Logical Scaffolding of Russell's Theory of Descriptions' *The Philosophical Review,* vol. 63, (1954).

Campbell, G. *Dissertation on Miracles. Containing an Examination of the Principles Advanced by David Hume in an Essay on Miracles,* Edinburgh: William Creech, 1762; (2nd ed. with additions 1797).

Campbell, R., 'Proper Names' *Mind,* vol. 77, (1968).

Campbell, R., review of Linsky, L. *Referring, Mind,* vol. 77, 1968).

Carey, Rosalind, Ongley, John *Historical dictionary of Bertrand Russell's philosophy* (Lanham: Scarecrow Press, 2009).

Carnap, R. *Logical Syntax of Language* eng. Tr. (London: Routledge & Kegan, Paul, 1937).

Carnap, R., *Meaning and Necessity,* (Chicago: University of Chicago Press, 1947).

Cartwright, R. L., 'Negative Existentials', *The Iournal of Philosophy,* vol. 57 (1960).

Cassin, C., 'Russell's Discussion of Meaning and Denotation: a Re-examination' in Klemke.

Cassin, C., 'Russell's Distinction Between the Primary and the Secundary Occurence of Definite Descriptions' in Klemke.

Caton, C. E., (ed.) *Philosophy and Ordinary Language* (Urbana: University of Illinois Press, 1963).

Caton C. E, 'Strawson on Referring' *Mind, n.s.* X, 68, 1959, pp. 539-544 reprinted in Klemke

Chalmers, Melanie and Nicholas Griffin,'s *Russell's Marginalia in his copy of Bradley's Principles of Logic,* Russell vol.17 (1997) N. 1, 1-96.

Chinol, E., *Il pensiero di S.T.* Coleridge (Napoli, Liguori, 1953).

Church, A., 'A Formulation of the Logic of Sense and Denotation' in P. Henle, H. M. Kallen, S. K. Langer (eds.) *Structures Method and Meaning*(New York: The Liberal art Press, 1951).

Church, A., 'The Need for Abstract Entities in Semantic Analysis' in J. Katz and J. Fodor (eds*.)*, *The Structures of Language,* (Englewood Cliffs: Prentice Hall, 1964).

Christensen, N. E., 'Logical Truth', *Mind,* vol. 263, (1957), 395-397.

Coleridge, S. T., *Inquiring Spirit. A New Presentation of Coleridge from his Published and Unpublished Prose Writing (*ed. by K. Coburn) (London: Routledge & Kegan Paul, 1951).

Coleridge, S. T., *The Notebooks of S. T. Coleridge* ed. by K. Coburn, 2 vols. (Princeton: Princeton University Press,1957-62).

Coleridge, S. T., *The Philosophical Lectures of S. T. Coleridge,* ed. by K. Coburn (London: 1949.new ed. London: The pilot press, 2009).

Coleridge, S. T., *The Friend, originally published* in 28 parts from June 1st 1809 to march 15th, reprinted London:1969)

Coleridge, S.T., *Aids to Reflection,*(London, Taylor and Hessey1825).

Coleridge, S. *T., Table Talk* (London, John Murray, 1836; other edition by T. Ash (London: T. Ash, 1923).

Coleridge, S. T., *Biographia Literaria* (Oxford: Clarendon Press, 1907).

Conrad, Joseph, *The Duel*, in: *A Set of Six* (London: Methuen & Co., 1908, pp. 245-334).

Cornman, 'On the Relevance of Linguistic Reference to Ontology' *The journal of Philosophy*, vol. 66, (1969).

Daly, C. B., 'Logical Positivisms, Metaphysics and Ethics in L. Wittgenstein' *Irish Theological Quarterly,* vol. 23 (1956).

Danto, A. C., 'A Note on Expressions of the Referring Sort' *Mind,* vol. 67, (1958).

Dennon, L., 'Bibliography of the Writings of Bertrand Russell to 1944' in P. A. Schilpp.

De Quincey. Th., *Collected Writings* (ed. by D. Masson, 14 vols., (London: Adam and Charles Black,1897).

De Quincey, Th., *Philosophical* Writers(London, Edward Moxon & Co, 1856).

Descartes, *Discours de la méthode* : texte et commentaire en regard / L. Meynard (Paris: Foucher; [s.d.]

Deschamps, P., *La formation de la pensée de Coleridge,* 1772-1804 (Paris: Librairie José Corti, 1964).

Donagan, A.,'Recent Criticisms of Russell's Analysis of Existence, *Analysis,* vol. 12, (1951-52).

Donnellan, K. S., 'Reference and Definite Descriptions' *The Philosophical Review,* vol. 75, (1966).

Edwards, P., 'Bertrand Russell's Doubts About Induction' in A. G. N. Flew. (ed.) *Essays in Conceptual* Analysis (London: MacMillan, 1956).

Feibleman, J. K., *Inside the Great Mirror. A Critical Examination of the Philosophy of Bertrand Russell, Wittgenstein and their Followers,*(The Hague, Martinus Nijhoff, 1958).

Feinberg, B., (ed.) *A Detailed Catalogue of the Archives of Bertrand Russell* (London: Thames and Hudson, 1967).

Findlay, J. N., 'Is There Knowledge by Acquaintance?', *Aristotelian Society Supplement,* vol. 23 (1949).

Findlay, J. N., *Meinong's Theory of Objects and Values,* (Oxford: Clarendon Press, 1963).

Fitch, F. B., 'The Problem of the Morning Star and the Evening Star' *Philosophy of Science,* vol. 23, (1949).

Flew, A. G. N., (ed.) *Essays in Conceptual Analysis* (London: Macmillan & Co, 1956).

Frege, Gottlob, Über Sinn und Bedeutung' in Zeitschrift für Philosophie und Philosophische Kritik, 100, 1982 pp. 25-50 in Max Black and Peter Geach eds., 1952 *translations from the Philosophical Writings of Gottlob Frege* (Oxford: Basil Blackwell, 1952).

Frege, G., 'The Thought' trans. from German by A. M. and Marcelle Quinton, *Mind,* vol. 65, (1956).

Frege, G., *Philosophical Writings* (ed. by P. Geach and M. Black) (Oxford: Blackwell, 1952).

Frege, G. 'Meaning and Meaninglessness' in Max Black and Peter Geach eds. *Translations from the Philosophical Writings of Gottlob Frege* (Oxford, Basil Blackwell, 1952).

Fritz, C. A., *Bertrand Russell's Construction of the External World,* (London: Routledge & Kegan Paul.1952).

Gale, R. M., 'Strawson's Restricted Theory of Referring' *The Philosophical Quarterly,* vol. 20, (1970).

Gale, R., 'Leonard Linsky, *Referring*' (review) *Journal of Philosophy,* vol. 66, (1969).

Geach, P., 'Russell's Theory of Descriptions' *Analysis,* vol. 10, (1950).

Geach, P., 'Russell on Meaning and Denoting', *Analysis,* vol. 19, (1958-59), reprinted in Klemke.

Geach, P. *Reference and Generality* (Ithaca: Cornell University Press,1962).

Geach, P., 'Referring Expressions Again', *Analysis,* vol. 2.4, (1963-64).

Geach, P., 'What Are Referring Expressions' in *Analysis,* vol. 23, 1962-63.

Götlind, Bertrand Russell's Theory of Causation (Upsala: Almqvist & Wiksels, 1952).

Gram, M. S., 'Ontology and the Theory of Descriptions' in Klemke.

Grave, S. A., *The Scottish Philosophy of Common Sense* (Oxford: Clarendon Press, 1960).

Green, Th. H., *Prolegomena to Ethics,* (3rd ed.). (Oxford: Clarendon Press, 1890).

Green, Th. H., Introduction to Hume's Treatise on Human Nature, 1885 repr. In Works of Thomas Hill Green ed. By R.L. Nettleship (Cambridge: Cambridge University Press, 2011) pp. 1-300; reprinted on line, 2012).

Grelling, K., 'Realism and Logic: an Investigation of Russell's Metaphysics', *The Monist,* vol. 39 (1929).

Griffin, J., *Wittgenstein's Logical Atomism,* (Oxford: Oxford University Press, 1964).

Grimm, R. N., 'Names and Predicables', *Analysis,* vol. 26, (1966).

Gross, B., *Analytic Philosophy: An Historical Introduction* (New York: MacMillan, 1970).

Hall, E., "The Extralinguistic Reference of Language (I)' in *Mind,* vol. 52, 1943.

Hall, E., 'The Extralinguistic Reference of Language (II)' *Mind,* vol. 53 (1944).

Hart, H. L. A., 'Is there Knowledge by Acquaintance?', *Aristotelian Society Supplement,* vol. 23, (1949).

Hay, W. N., 'Bertrand Russell on the Justification of Induction', *Philosophy of Science,* vol. 17 (1950).

Hazlitt, W., *Complete Works* (ed. by P. P. Howe) 21 vols. (London:J.M. Dent & Sons, 1931).

Heath, A. E., 'The Principle of Parsimony and Ethical Neutrality', *The Monist,* vol. 29, (1919).

Hempel, C., 'Some Remarks on "Facts" and Propositions', *Analysis,* vol. 2, (1935).

Hempel, C., 'On the Logical Positivists' Theory of Truth', *Analysis,* vol. 2 (1935).

Hempel, C., 'On Russell's Phenomenological Constructionism', *The Journal of Philosophy,* vol. 63 (1966).

Hicks, G. D., 'The Philosophical Researches of Meinong', *Mind,* vol. 31 (1922).

Hochberg, H., 'Peano, Russell and Logicism' in Klemke. Hochberg, H., 'Descriptions, Scope and Identity' in Klemke.

Hochberg, H., 'Russell's Reduction of Arithmetic to Logic' in Klemke.

Hochberg, H., 'On Referring and Asserting', *Philosophical Studies,* vol. 20 (1969).

Hochberg, H., 'Strawson, Russell and the King of France', *Philosophy of Science,* vol. 37 (1970).

Hochberg, H., 'Things and Descriptions' in Klemke.

Honderich, E. D. R., 'Logic and Knowledge' *Philosophy,* vol. 37 (1962).

Honderich, E. D. R., 'On the Theory of Descriptions', *Proceedings of the Aristotelian Society,* vol. 69 (1968-69).

Houang, F., *Le Neohegelianisme en Angleterre,*(Paris: Vrin, 1954).

Howard, C., *Coleridge's Idealism. A Study of its Relationship to Kant and to the Cambridge Platonists* (Boston: Richard Badger, 1924).

Hughes, G. E., 'Is There Knowledge by Acquaintance?', *Aristotelian Society Supplement,* vol. 23 (1949).

Jacobson, A., 'Russell and Strawson on Referring', in Klemke.

Jackson, R., 'Critical Notice of Meinong's Theory of Objects', by J. N. Findlay, Mind, vol. 43 (1934).

Jacques, J. H., 'The Appeal to Common Sense', *The Listener*, vol. 63 (1960).

Jager, R. E., 'Russell's Denoting Complex', *Analysis*, vol. 20, (1959-60).

Jager, R. E., The Development of Bertrand Russell's Philosophy (London: George Allen & Unwin 1972).

Jeffreys, M. D. W., 'Ockam's Razor: a Reply', *Nada*, vol. 31 (1954).

Harold. Joachim, *The Nature of Truth* (Oxford: Oxford University Press,1906).

Johnson Darroch, Sandra *Garsington revisited: the legenf of Lady Ottoline Morrell brough up-to-date*(Herts, England: John Libbey Pub., 2017)

Jourdain, PH. E. B., 'The Logical Significance of Ockam's Razor',*The Monist*, vol. 29 (1919).

; Philip E. B Jourdain, *The philosophy of Mr. B*rtr*nd R*ss*ll : with an appendix of leading passages from certain other* work (, Abingdon, Oxon: Routledge, 2013).

Kant, Immanuel *Prolegomena zu einer jeden künftigen Metaphysik, die als Wissenschaft wird auftreten können,*(F. Meiner Verlag, Hamburg 1951),

Keen C. N., 'The Interaction of Russell and Bradley' *Russell*, The Journal of the Bertrand Russell Archives, vol. 3 (1971).pp. 7-11

Khol, M., 'Bertrand Russell on Vagueness', *Australasian Journal of Philosophy*, vol. 47 (1969).

Kirwan, C., 'On the Connotation and Sense of Proper Names', *Mind*, vol. 77 (1968).

Klemke, E. D., (ed.) *Essays on Bertrand Russell* (Urbana: University of Illinois Press,1970).

Klemke, E. D., 'Logic and Ontology' in Klemke.

Kuhn,Th. *The structure of Scientific Revolutions,* (Chicago:The University of Chicago Press, 1962).

Laird, J., 'The Law of Parsimony" *The Monist*, vol. 29 (1919).

Laird, l. 'On certain Russell's views concerning the human mind' in P. A. Schilpp, *The Philosophy of Bertrand Russell,* (pp. 293-316).

Leibniz, G. W. F., Philosophische Werke, ed. by Gerhardt (Berlin: Weidmannsche Buchhandlung, 1875-1890).

Lejevsky, C., 'A Re-examination of the Russellian Theory of Descriptions', *Philosophy*, vol. 35 (1960).

Lenzen, V. F., 'Bertrand Russell at Harvard, 1914', *Russell*, vol. 3 (1971).

Lewis, I. C. *An Analysis of Knowledge and Valuation* (La Salle: Open Court 1946).

Lewis, J., Bertrand Russell, Philosopher and Humanist (London: George Allen & Unwin, 1968).

Linsky, L., Semantics and the Philosophy of Language, (Urbana, University of Illinois Press, 1952).

Linsky, L., 'Descriptions and the Antinomy of the Name-Relation', *Mind,* vol. 61 (1952).

Linsky, L., 'Substitutivity and Descriptions', *Journal of Philosophy*, vol. 63 (1966).

Linsky, L., *Referring* (London: Routledge & Kegan Paul, 1967).

Linsky, L., 'Reference, Essentialism and Modality', *Journal of Philosophy*, vol. 66 (1969).

Linsky, L., 'Reference and Referents', in Klemke.

Linsky, L., Reference and Modality (Oxford: Oxford University Press, 1971).

Lucas, B. J., 'Moore's Influence on Russell', *Russell*, vol. I (1971).

Macdonald, M., 'Language and Reference', *Analysis*, vol. 4 (1933).

Macdonald, M., 'Russell and McTaggart', *Philosophy*, vol. 11 (1936).

Malcolm, N., 'Defending Common Sense', *Philosophical Review*, vol. 58 (1949).

Malcolm, N., 'Russell's Human Knowledge', *Philosophical Review*, vol. 59, 1950.

Malcolm, N., *Knowledge and Certainty* (Englewood Cliffs: Prentice Hall, 1964).

Marcus, R. B., 'Extensionality', *Mind*, vol. 69 (1960).

Martin, R. M., 'On the Berkelev-Russell Theory of Proper Names', *Philosophy and Phenomenological Research*, vol. 13 (1952-3).

Martin Werner, Bertrand Russell : a bibliography of his writings = Eine Bibliographie seiner Schriften, 1895-1976, (, Munchen: K. G. Saur, 1981).

McGuinness, B. F., Von Wright, *Wittgenstein and his Cambridge Friends. Letters to Russell, Keynes and Moore*, (Oxford: Oxford University Press, 1995).

McLendon, J. H., 'Has Russell Answered Hume?', *Journal of Philosophy*, vol. 49 (1952).

Meinong, A., 'Uber Gegensdndstheorie' in *Gesammelte Abhandlungen, I* (Leipzig: Felix Meiner, 1913).

Michaelis, Anne L., 'The Conception of Possibility in Meinong's "Gegensdndstheorie"', *Philosophy and Phenomenological Research*, vol. 3 (1942).

Mill, J. Stuart, Examination of Sir William Hamilton's Philosophy (London: Longmans, Green1865).

Mill, J. Stuart, '*On Bentham and Coleridge*, (ed. and with an introduction by F. R. Leavis), (London: Chatto & Windus 1967).

Moore, G. E., 'The Nature of Judgement' *Mind*, vol. 8 (1899).

Moore, George E. 'External and Internal Relations' *Proceedings* of the *Aristotelian Society,* vol. XX (1919-20) pp. 40-62, repr. in *Philosophical Studies* (London: Kegan Paul, 1922) pp. 276-309.

Moore, G.E.. *The Foundations of Mathematics, and other Essays,* (London: Routledge & Kegan Paul, 1931).

Moore, G. E., Some Main Problems of Philosophy (London: George Allen & Unwin, 1953).

Moore, G. E., 'Russell's Theory of Descriptions', in P. A. Schilpp

Moore, G. E., Philosophical Essays (London: George Allen & Unwin, 1959.).

Moore, G.E. *Principia Ethica.* (Cambridge: Cambridge University Press, 1903).

Morris, Engels., 'Isomorphism and Linguistic Waste', *Mind*, vol. 74 (1965).

Mugnai, M., 'Bertrand Russell and the Problem of Relations in Leibniz', *Rivista di Filosofia*, vol. 64 (1973).

Muirhead, J. H., 'How Hegel came to England', *Mind*, vol. 36 (1927).

Muirhead, J. H., Coleridge as Philosopher (London: George Allen & Unwin, 1930).

Muirhead, J. H., The Platonic Tradition in Anglo-Saxon Philosophy (London: Routledge, 1931).

Muirhead, J. H 'Past and Present in Contemporary Philosophy' in *Contemporary British Philosophy,*(London: Routledge 1924,

Nagel, E., 'Mr. Russell on Meaning and Truth', *Journal of Philosophy*, vol., 38 (1941).

Nakhnikian, George, *Bertrand Russell's philosophy* (London: Duckworth, 1974).

Newberry, J., 'Russell in 1916', *Russell*, vol. 2 (1971).

Nielsen, Kai 'Broad's Conception of Critical and Speculative Philosophy Dialectica, Vol. 48, No. 1 (1994), pp. 47-64

O'Connor, D. J., *A Critical History of Western Philosophy* (New York: The Free Press, 1964).

O'Hara. G., 'Ockam's Razor Today', *Philosophical Studies*, vol. 12 (1963).

O'Keeffe, J.A, *An Essay on the Progress of Understanding,*(London: V. Griffiths, 1795).

Orsini, G. N., *Coleridge and German ldealism* (Carbondale: Southern Illinoi University press, 1969.

Oswald, J., An Appeal to Common Sense on Behalf of Religion (Edinburgh: Alexander Kincaid, 1766).

Pap, A., Elements of Analytic Philosophy (New York: Mac Millan, 1949).

Pap, A., 'Philosophical Analysis, Translations, Schemas and the Regularity Theory of Causation', *Journal, of Philosophy*, vol. 49 (1952).

Passmore, John *A Hundred Years of Philosophy* (Harmondsworth: Penguin Books,1968)

Passmore, J., 'Russell and Bradlev' in Brown, R., Rollins, C. D. eds., *Contemporary Philosophy in Australia* (London: George Allen & Unwin1969).

Peacock, Th. *The Halliford Edition of the Works of Th.L. Peacock*, ed. by H. F. B. Brett-Smith and C. E. Jones, 10 vols (London Macmillan 1924-34).

Peacock, TL. L., The Novels of Th. L. Peacock, edited by D. Garnett, 2 vols.(London: Rupert Hart Davies 1948, 2nd ed 1963.

Peacock, Thomas. L. *Melincourt* (London: Rupert Hart Davies, 1963).

Peacock, Thomas. L Complete Novels (London: Rupert Hart Davies, 1963).

Pears, D. F., 'Logical Atomism: Russell and Wittgenstein', in G. Ryle (ed.) *The Revolution in Philosophy* (London: Macmillan, 1956).

Pears, D. F., *Bertrand Russell and the British Tradition in Philosophy* (London: Collins,1968).

Pears, D. F., (ed.) Bertrand Russell (Garden City: Doubleday 1972).

Pears, D. F., (ed.) Bertrand Russell, *Logical Atomism,*(London: W. M. Collins, 1972).

Pitt, J., 'With Russell at the Archives', *Russell,* vol. 2, (1971).

Popper, K. R. *The Logic of Scientific Discovery,* Engl tr. (Abingdon-on-Thames: Routledge, 1959). New edition London: Routledge Classics, 2002).

Price, H. H., *Perception* (London: Methuen, 1932).

Prior, A. N., 'Existence in Lesniewski and Russell', in Crossley, J. N. E. A. Emerson, C. A. Meredith, and R. T. Richter, *Formal Systems and Recursive Functions,*(Amsterdam: North-Holland Publishing,1965).

Pritchard, H. A., 'Mr. Bertrand Russell on Our Knowledge of the External World', *Mind,* vol. 24 (1915).

Pritchard, H. A., *Knowledge and Perception,* (Oxford: Oxford University Press. 1950).

Pucelle, J., *L'idealisme en Angleterre, de Coleridge a Bradley* (Neuchatel: Éditions de la Baçonnière 1955).

Quine, W. V. O., *From a Logical Point of View,* (Cambridge, Mass.: Harvard University Press,1951).

Quine, W. V. O., *World and Object,* (New York: MIT Press, 1960).

Quine, W. V. O., 'Russell's Ontological Development', *Journal of Philosophy,* vol. 63, (1966): repr. in Klemke.

Quine, W. V. O., 'An Appraisal of Bertrand Russell's Philosophy in D. F. Pears, (ed.) *Bertrand Russell.*

Quine, W. V. O., *The Ways of Paradox,* (New York: Random House, 1966).

Quinton, A. M., 'Contemporary British Philosophy', in D. J. O'Connor (ed.) *A Critical History of Western Philosophy,* (New York: Free Press of Glencoe, 1964).

Quinton, A. M., 'Absolute Idealism' Dawes Hick's lecture on Philosophy, British Academy, 1971, *Proceedings of the British Academy,* vol. 57, London: 1972).

Ramsden, Eames E., 'The Consistency of Russell's Realism', *Philosophy and Phenomenological Research,* vol. 27, (1966-7).

Ramsden Eames, E., *Bertrand Russell's Theory of Knowledge* (London: George Allen & Unwin, 1969).

Ramden Eames, E., 'Russell's Study of Meinong', *Russell,* vol. 4, (1971-72).

Ramsey, F. P., *The Foundations of Mathematics and Other Logical Essays* (London: Routledge & Kegan Paul, 1931).

Ramsey, F.P. 'Facts and Propositions' in *The Foundations of Mathematics and Other logical Essays*

Ready, W., *Necessary Russell* (Toronto: Copp Clark, 1969).

Ready, W., 'Donors', in *Russell,* vol. 4, 1971.

Recanati, François, *Literal Meaning* (Cambridge: Cambridge University Press, 2004).

Reeves, J. W., 'The Origin and Consequences of the Theory of Descriptions' *Proceedings of the Aristotelian Society,* vol. 14, (1933-34).

Reid, Thomas, *An Inquiry into the Human Mind on the Principles of Common,* Sense, *in The Works of Thomas Reid ed.by William Hamilton* (Hildesheim: Georg Olms, 1895).

Reid, Th., *Essays on the Intellectual Powers of Man,* 1785, Menston Scholar Press, 1971, Facsimile reprint of the Ist edition (Edinburgh: J. Bell and G. Robinson, 1785).

Reid, Th., *Essays on the Power of the Human Mind; to* which are prefixed an *Essay on Quantity and an Analysis of Aristotle's Logic,* in three volumes (Edinburgh: Ogle, Debrett, and Creech, 1785 republished in 1819).

Reid, Th., *Works,* edited by Sir W. Hamilton, 2 vols. 1846-63 (Edinburgh: Thomas Constable 1872).

Reid, Th., *Th. Reid on the Distinction between Sensation and Perception,* 1785, in *A Source Book in the History of Psychology,* (Cambridge, Cambridge UP. 1965).

Reid, Th., *Philosophical Works,* with Notes and Supplementary Dissertations by Sir W. Hamilton (Hildesheim: Olms-Weidmann 1967 (anastatic reprint).

Reid, Th., 'Of the Objects of Perception' and First of Primary and Secundary Qualities', in *Berkeley's Principles of Human Knowledge,* Belmont, 1968.

Reid, TH., "A Common Sense Approach to the Foundations of Knowledge in *The Foundations of Knowledge,* (Englewood Cliffs: Prentice Hall, 1970).

Reimer, M. and A. Bezuidenhout, *Descriptions and Beyond* (Oxford, New York: Oxford University press, 2004).

Riverso, E., *Il Pensiero di Bertrand Russell* (Naples: Istituto Editoriale del Mezzogiorno, 1958).

Rogers, C. F., 'Ockam's Razor', *Theology,* vol. 40 (1940).

Rosaye, Jean Paul, *F.H.Bradley et l'idealisme britannique. Les années de formation (1865-1876),* (Arras: Artois, Presse Université, 2020).

Ruja, H. 'A Selective, Classified Bertrand Russell Bibliography' in Pears (ed.)

Russell, B. *An Essay on the Foundations of Geometry* (Cambridge: Cambridge University Press, 1897).

Russell, B. 'On the Relations of Number and Quantity', *Mind, v.* 6, (1896), 326-341).

Russell, B. *A Critical Exposition of the Philosophy of Leibniz : with an appendix of Leading passages* (Cambridge: Cambridge University Press, 1900) 2nd ed. with a new preface (London: George Allen & Unwin, 1937).

Russell, B., 'The Logic of Relations' *Journal of Mathematics,* 7 (1900-1), pp. 115-148 reprinted later in *Logic and Knowledge.*

Russell, B. 'On Denoting' Mind, XIV, 1905, pp. 473-493, reprinted in *Logic and knowledge* pp. 39-56).

Russell, B. 'The Monistic Theory of Truth' in *Philosophical Essays* (London: Longmans, Green & Co, 1910).

Russell, B. 'Knowledge by Acquaintance and Knowledge by Description', Proc. Arist. Soc., V, II, (1910), pp. 108-128, reprinted in *Mysticism and Logic,*

Mind, XIV, 1905, pp. 473-493, reprinted in *Logic and knowledge* (London: George Allen & Unwin, 1956).

Russell, B., 'On The Nature of Acquaintance' *The Monist, v.* XXIV (1914), pp. 1-16; 161-187; 435-453; reprinted in *Logic and Knowledge,* pp. 125-174).

Russell, B., *Our Knowledge of the External World* (London: George Allen B. Russell, *Introduction to Mathematical Philosophy* (London: Allen & Unwin, 1919).

Russell, B. 'On Scientific Method in Philosophy' in *Mysticism and Logic, pp. 97-124*

Russell, B., *Roads to Freedom* (London: George Allen& Unwin, 1918,new ed. 1949).

Russell, B. 'The Logic of Relations' *The Journal of Mathematics,* 7 (1900-1), pp. 115-148 reprinted later in *Logic and Knowledge.*

Russell, B., *The Practice and Theory of Bolshevism* (London: George Allen & Unwin, 1920).

Russell, B., 'The Philosophy of logical Atomism' in *Logic and Knowledge. Ed. By Marsch Robert C.* (London: Allen & Unwin, 1956).

Russell, B. Logical Atomism, in *Contemporary British Philosophy*, Personal Statements, First series (London: George Allen & Unwin,1924) pp. 356-383;repr.in *Logic and Knowledge* pp.335 ff).

Russell, B. 'Whitehead and Principia Mathematica',*Mind,* 57, (1948, pp. 137 ff).

Russell, B. *Power a Social Analysis (* London: Allen & Unwin 1938, new ed. 1948).

Russell, B. *My Philosophical Development* (London: Allen and Unwin,1959, 2nd ed. Unwin Books 1975).

Russell, B. 'My Mental Development' in The *Philosophy of Bertrand Russell*, ed. By Paul. Arthur Schilpp The Library of Living philosophers, vol. V.(La Salle: Open Court, 1971, pp.1-20).

Russell, B. *The Problems of Philosophy* (London: William and Norgate, 1912 (Oxford: Oxford University press E book 2001).

Russell, B. *The Autobiography of Bertrand Russell'*3 vols. (London: George Allen and Unwin, 1967-1968-1969).

RUSSELL, The Journal of the Bertrand Russell Archives, vols. 1-24, 1971-1977).

Ryle, G., 'Systematically Misleading Expressions', reprinted in *Essays in Logic and Language,* ed. by A. G. N. Flew, (Oxford: Blackwell, 1950).

Ryle, G., 'The Theory of Meaning', repr.in Caton, (ed.). *Philosophy and Ordinary Language.*

Santucci, A. (ed.) *Scienza e filosofia scozzese nell'età di Hume* (Bologna: Il Mulino 1976).

Scheer, R. K, 'Verification and the Performatory Theorv of Truth' *Mind,* vol, 69, n. 276, 1960. p. 568).

Schilpp, P. A., (ed.) *The Philosophy of Bertrand Russell,* (La Salle, Ill., Open Court, 1944).

Sciacca, M. F., *La Filosofia di Tommaso Reid,* (Milano: Marzorati,1963).

Schlick, M., 'Facts and Propositions', *Analysis,* vol. 2 (1935).

Schlick, M., 'Il fondamento gnoseologico' in *il Neoempirismo,* edited by A. Pasquinelli, (Turin: UTET, 1969).

Shoemaker, S., 'Logical Atomism and Language', *Analysis,* vol. 20 (1949).

Schoenman, R., (ed.) *Bertrand Russell, Philosopher of the Century* (London: Allen & Unwin,1967).

Searle, J., 'Proper Names' *Mind,* vol. 67 (1958), reprinted in Caton.

Searle, J., 'Russell's Objections to Frege's Theory of Sense and Reference' *Analysis,* vol. 18 (1957-8).

Segre, U., 'Il pensiero etico-politico di Russell', *Rivista Critica di Storia della Filosofia,* vol. 8 (1953).

Shearn, M., 'Russell's Analysis of Existence', *Analysis,* vol. 11 (1950-1).

Shearn, M., 'Wittgenstein and Russell's Theory of Types', *Analysis,* vol. 11 (1950-1).

Simpson, Th. Moro, 'A Note on Sense and Denotation' *Nous, vol.* 1 (1967).

Smart, J. J.C, Whitehead and Russell's Theory of Types',

I *Analysis,* vol. 10 (1950).

Smart, J. J. C., *Philosophy and Scientific Realism* (London: Routledge & Kegan Paul, 1963).

Smiley, T., 'Sense without Denotation', in *Analysis,* vol. 20 (1959-60).

Snyder, Alice D., *Coleridge on Logic and Learning,* with Selections from the unpublished Mss. (New Haven: Yale University Press, 1929).

Snyder, Alice D., *S. T. Coleridge's Treatise on Method,* (New Haven, Yale University Press, 1934).

Sprigge, T. L. S., 'Internal and External Properties', *Mind,* vol. 71 (1962).

Stace, W. 'Russell's neutral monism', in A. Schilpp (ed.) *The philosophy of Bertrand Russell,* pp. 351-385.

Stevenson, C. L., Some Relations between Philosophy and the Study of Language', *Analysis,* vol. 8 (1947).

Stewart, D., *Elements of the Philosophy of the Human Mind,* Edinburgh: William Creech 1792).

Stirling, James H. *The Secret of Hegel* (London: Longmans & Green 1855).

Stout, G. F., 'Alleged Self Contradictions in the Concept of Relation', *Proceedings of the Aristotelian Society,* 1 (1901).

Stout, G. F., 'Bradley's Theory of Relations', in *Studies in Philosophy and Psychology* (London: MacMillan, 1930).

Strachey, O., 'Mr. Russell and Some Recent Criticisms of his Views', *Mind,* vol. 24 (1915).

Strawson, P. F., 'Truth', *Analysis, vol.* 10 (1949).

Strawson, P. F., 'On Referring', *Mind,* vol. 59 (1950), reprinted in Copi and in Klemke.

Strawson, P. F., *Introduction to Logical Theory,* (London: Methuen & Co. 1961).

Strawson, P. F., 'A Reply to Mr. Sellars', *Philosophical Review,* vol. 63 (1954).

Strawson, P. F., *Individuals,* (London: Methuen & Co, 1959).

Strawson, P. F., 'Identifying Reference and Truth Values', in Klemke.

Stuart Mill, John. 'Bentham' *London and Westminster Review,* August 1838 and 'Coleridge' in March 1840 issue of the same journal the two essays were brought together in a small volume entitled *Mill on Bentham and Coleridge* with an introduction by F.R. Leavis, (London: Chatto & Windus, 1967. See pp. 99 ff. of this edition.

Sutter, R., 'Russell's Refutation of Meinong in "On Denoting" *Philosophy and Phenomenological Research,* vol. 27 (1967).

Swanson, Carolyn, *Reburial of Nonexistents Reconsidering the Meinong-Russell Debate* (Amsterdam, New York: Rodopi, 2011).

Tarsky, A., 'The Semantic Conception of Truth and the Foundations of Semantics', *Philosophy and Phenomenological Research,* vol. 4 (1944).

Thorburn, W. H., 'Ockham's Razor', *Mind,* vol. 24, 1915.

Thorburn, W. H., 'The Myth of Ockam's Razor' *Mind, vol.* 27 (1918).

Turner, J. E., 'Mr. Strachey's Defence of Mr. Russell's Theory' *Mind,* vol. 24 (1915).

Urmson, J.O., *Philosophical Analysis* (Oxford: Oxford University Press, 1956 2nd 1967).

Ushenko, P. A. 'Russell's critique of empiricism', in P.A. Schilpp The philosophy of Bertrand Russell, pp. 385-41).

Vallicella, William A. 'Monism and the Vindication of Bradley's Regress', *Dialectica* 2002, Vol. 56 N. (2002) p. 3-35).

Veath, H., 'The Philosophy of Logical Atomism: a Realism *Manqué'* in Klemke.

Wisdom, J. *Logical Constructions, Mind* 40 (158):188-216 (1931).

Von Sicard, H., Ockam's Razor', *Nada,* vol. 30 (1953). Vuillemin, J., *La première philosophie de Russell,* (Paris: Éditions du Seuil 1968).

Wang, Hao, 'Russell and His Logic' *Ratio,* vol. 7 (1965).

Warnock, G. *J.,English Philosophy Since,* 1900 (Oxford: Oxford University Press, 1969).

Watling, J., *Bertrand Russell* (Edinburgh: Oliver & Boyd, 1970).

Weitz, M. 'Analysis and the Unity of Russell's Philosophy' in P.A. Schilpp (ed.), *The Philosophy of Bertrand Russell,* pp. 55-121).

Wellek, R., *I. Kant in England,* 1793-1838 (Princeton: Princeton University Press, 1931).

Wellek, R., 'Coleridge's Philosophy and Criticism', in *The English Romantic Poets* ed.by George McLean Harper (New York: MacMillan 1917).

Wells, D. A., 'Basic Propositions in Ayer and Russell?, in Writings *Journal of Philosophy,* vol. 51 (1954).

Werner, Martin, *Bertrand Russell: A bibliography of his writings _ Eine bibliographie seiner Schriften 1895-1976* (Munchen: K.G. Saur 1981)

White, A. R., 'The "Meaning" of Russell's Theory of Descriptions' *Analysis,* vol. 20 (1959-60).

Winkelmann, E., *Coleridge und die Kantische Philosophie* (Hildesheim: Georg Olms Verlag, 1933).

Winslade, W. J., 'Russell's Theory of Relations', in Klemke.

Wisdom, J., 'Logic & Construction',*Mind*, Volume XLIII, n169, 1934, pp.120–122).

Wisdom, J. 'Logical Constructions', *Mind*, n.s. 40 pp. 189-216, 460-475. (1931). the essay continues in Mind, 41, (1932), pp. 441-464 and *Mind*, 42 (1933), pp. 43-66 and 186-202).

Wittgenstein, L., *Tractatus Logico-Philosophicus,* Engl. tr. (London: kegan Paul, 1921).

Wittgenstein, L., *Philosophical Investigations,* (Oxford: Blackwell, 1953).

Wittgenstein, L.*Notebooks* 1914-16 (Oxford: Blackell, 1961).

Wollheim Richard., *F. H. Bradley* (Harmondsworth: Penguin Books, 1969)

Wollheim, R., 'F. H. Bradley' in G. Ryle (ed.) *The Revolution in Philosophy* (London: MacMillan, 1956).

Wolniewicz, B., 'A difference between Russell's and Wittgenstein's Logical Atomism' Kongress (XIV) Internationaler fur Philosophie, Wien, 2-9 Sept. 1968, (Akten,Wien, 1968).

INDEX OF NAMES

The names Russell and Bradley, which recur very frequently in the text, do not appear in this index.

Printed by
Rotomail Italia
February 2024